Yellowstone

By David Rains Wallace

A Natural and Human History
Yellowstone National Park
Idaho, Montana, and Wyoming

Produced by the
Division of Publications
Harpers Ferry Center
National Park Service

U.S. Department of the Interior
Washington, D.C.

National Park Handbooks

Yellowstone National Park has more active geothermal features than the rest of the world and is
part of one of the largest and most intact temperate
ecosystems on Earth. This handbook will help you
understand the values and significance of this world-
renowned area and appreciate its wild nature.

The National Park Handbook series is published to
support National Park Service management programs and to promote the understanding and enjoyment of the more than 380 National Park System
sites, which preserve important parts of our nation's
natural and cultural inheritance. Handbooks are
sold at National Park System sites and can also be
purchased by mail from the Superintendent of Documents, U.S. Government Printing Office, Stop
SSOP, Washington, DC 20402-0001 or through the
internet at bookstore.gpo.gov. This is handbook
number 150.

Part 1

"Nature at Work As a Chemist"

The closest thing I've seen to what the Persian poet Omar Khayam called "the first Morning of Creation" must be Mud Volcano thermal field in Yellowstone's Hayden Valley. All the park's mudpots and fumaroles are strange, but these have an expansive grandeur very like an artist's imaginings of a fiery young Earth that fascinated me as a child. Often as I walked around the boardwalk with a park interpretive ranger, sulfurous steam clouds, bubbling multi-colored mud, and some poisonous green springholes were the only things in sight. A rising October moon seemed to shine coldly on a primeval world. The world even sounded primeval as water surged and hissed in the cavernous pool of Dragon's Mouth.

The sounds and sights would have seemed even stranger had I been there during one of the abrupt changes this thermal field sometimes undergoes. When explorer Nathaniel Langford encountered it in 1870, he heard "dull, thundering, booming sounds resembling the reports of distant artillery." The ground "shook and trembled," Langford reported. At that time the giant conical mudpot of Mud Volcano itself had only recently appeared, and, regularly, it erupted "dense masses of steam" that "burst forth like the smoke of burning gunpowder." It became so violent by 1898 it apparently blew itself out.

Subsidence of one explosive feature just leads to the emergence of another. The interpretive ranger showed me where a 10-foot-wide mudpot became a 30-foot-wide mudpot in a single month. Its mud bubbles were the size of Dantesque human heads—shiny gray objects that seethed and croaked hypnotically. While she was telling me how a ranger had discovered it accidentally, I began to feel strangely uncomfortable. The 200°F heat of the ground was starting to cook my feet.

Mud Volcano is so bizarre it might be on some lifeless, alien planet, but it is by no means lifeless. In fact, it probably is not unlike the environment in which life first appeared, because the oldest living things still thrive deep in its hot springs. They are single-celled organisms. They resemble the bacteria that cover the Earth's surface, but their metabolisms are so different that biologists recently created a new kingdom for them, the *Archaea*. Although invisible without high magnification, they teem in hot spring water so abundantly they create mudpots by metabolizing sulfur and water into rock-dissolving sulfuric acid. Yellowstone's thermal fields seem to recapitulate not only life's first appearance but its early development—as organisms first began metabolizing oxygen instead of sulfur.

At thermal fields like the Firehole River's, such aerobic organisms (so-named because they require oxygen) are conspicuous on the surface. As water flows from hot springs, mats of brilliant color appear, first yellow, then orange and green. These mats are colonies of photosynthetic bacteria and algae. Their ancient ancestors generated the atmosphere we live in. In the outflow of one geyser I also saw stringy whitish films, colonies of *Thermus aquaticus*, a non-photosynthetic bacterium. It is very like the bacteria covering our skins—with the crucial exception that *T. aquaticus* is adapted to live at temperatures as high as 176°F.

That I found myself so surprised at how fascinating Yellowstone's thermal features can be, was an embarrassing admission for an American. After all, Old Faithful Geyser is one of the United States' fundamental symbols. It ranks up there with Old Glory.

Since 1872, when Congress created Yellowstone National Park from the public domain in a vast rectangle of Wyoming, Montana, and Idaho territories, other aspects of the park have become symbolic. Its bears and other wildlife symbolize the freedom and wealth of a continent that seemed boundless to Old World colonists. Its monumental scenery, such as the Grand Canyon of the Yellowstone, symbolizes

Next pages: *Hot spring colors and shapes, such as those of Canary Spring, change more frequently at Mammoth Hot Springs than in most other park thermal basins. Rapid mineral buildup clogs underground plumbing, changing water circulation and hot spring activity.*

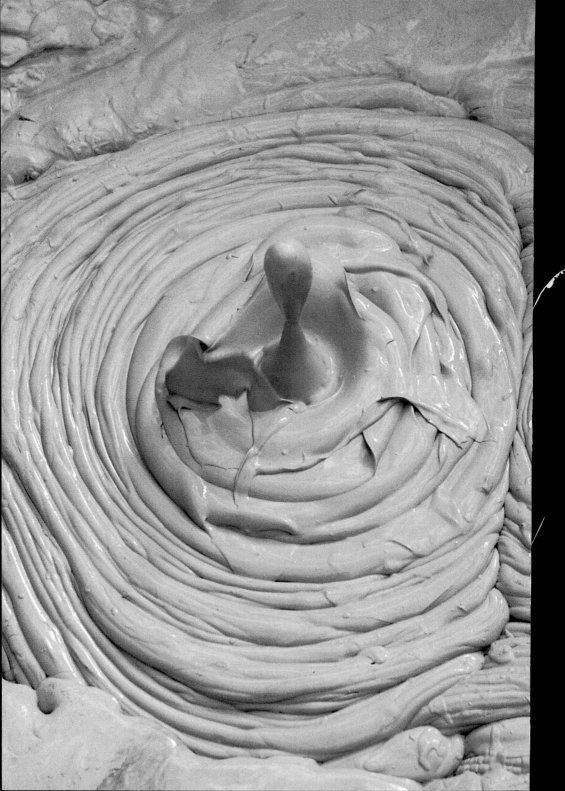

*Mudpots' activity may vary
with the season. Winter snows
tend to thin mud with water;
summer heat may thicken the
mud or dry up some features
completely.*

*Not only is Norris Geyser
Basin the hottest thermal area
in Yellowstone, but many of
its features are highly acidic.
Yet even here, these colorful
microbes thrive in some of
Earth's most extreme environments.*

the pride and aspirations of a relatively new nation. For many, Americans and non-Americans alike, Yellowstone itself is a symbol of America.

Yet such symbols do get crusted over with familiarity. Growing up without visiting the park, I had associated geysers, bears, and scenery with those grainy photos in encyclopedias. What I did grow up with was a vivid idea of Yellowstone as one of the last nearly intact remnants of the American wilderness. That idea so dominated my attitude toward the park that during my first visit I didn't even try to see the thermal features or the Grand Canyon of the Yellowstone. When at last I did see them, I realized I'd almost missed the heart of the place.

Civilization might have missed the heart of this place, too, except for a historical accident. Iceland's geysers had been known for centuries when Yellowstone became a park, and Italy's mudpots for millennia, but nobody had preserved them. Yellowstone's establishment as a national park depended on a new way of looking at such so-called "curiosities." Humans long had understood more about the transparent, mathematically predictable heavens than about this opaque, catastrophically changing Earth. The Earth remained the province of miner-craftsmen while astronomers like Galileo and Newton worked out laws of celestial motion. During the 18th century, however, as industrializing civilization increasingly needed minerals and energy, naturalists like James Hutton looked more systematically at rocks and mountains.

Such observations coalesced into the science of geology—and made the difference between how Iceland's geysers had been regarded and how Yellowstone's would be. Increased understanding of the nature of geysers led many to regard them not as alien and threatening but as attractive and alive with warm colors and memorable sounds and smells.

While 19th-century Americans prized Yellowstone's wonders for their curiosity, they also valued them as manifestations of natural processes that might expand human horizons. The 1870s saw the establishment of U.S. geological surveys as well as the park. One of Yellowstone's main explorers, Ferdinand Hayden, was a government geologist. Members of Congress would not have voted to preserve Yellowstone if it had seemed only an infernal amusement park. They were well aware of the deeper implications of all that steam rushing forth from the ground and water crashing over falls—such forces drove industrial development then. Geology was a cutting-edge science of the mid-19th century. Geology then was like space exploration would be to the mid-20th century, and the Yellowstone area was its Mars. Yellowstone was that faraway, alien place where theories could be tested by observing natural forces still at work in spectacularly pristine ways. "This noble deed may be regarded as a tribute from our legislators to science," Hayden wrote about the park's creation.

The new way of regarding the Earth was not confined to geologists and legislators. The fur trapper Joe Meek expressed it in rudimentary but vivid language in 1829. Meek likened one of Yellowstone's geyser basins to the industrial "city of Pittsburgh." Three young frontiersmen who explored the region 40 years later echoed Meek, calling one hot spring concentration "the chemical works."

Naturalist John Muir's reaction was similar in the 1880s. Although famous today as a conservationist and writer, Muir started out as a successful inventor. His description of Yellowstone's Midway Geyser Basin typifies how progressivism and geology combined in 19th-century perceptions. "These valleys at the heads of the great rivers may be regarded as laboratories or kitchens," Muir wrote, "in which, amid a thousand retorts and pots, we may see Nature at work as a chemist."

"Take a look into a few of the tertiary volumes of the grand geological library of the park," urged Muir, "and see how God writes history."

Yellowstone provided a particularly spectacular place to observe the interplay between two basic ways the Earth works—change and continuance. Early visitors had no trouble reading Yellowstone as a textbook of geological changes. In 1870 Army Lieutenant Gustavus C. Doane remarked how "one mountain succeeds another with precipitous ravines volcanic, rugged, and in many cases impassable, as if all the fusible parts of the mountains had melted and run away leaving a vast cinder behind." With its thermal basins and looming lava flows, Yellowstone looked like the arena of some ancient cataclysm. Yet Yellowstone also contained evidence of lengthy

Next page: *Great Fountain Geyser's sunset glow belies the power of its eruptions. Bursts range from 100-150 feet; rare superbursts blast water more than 200 feet into the air.*

THOMAS MORAN

Tiny human figures dramatize the size of Excelsior Geyser's pool. Massive eruptions reaching heights of over 300 feet occurred mostly during the 1800s. Today, Excelsior discharges over 4,000 gallons of water per minute into the Firehole River from its crater at the edge of Midway Geyser Basin.

stability. In that same paragraph Doane described a landscape possessing sylvan tranquillity: "The deep and narrow valleys were grassed and timbered, had sparkling streams and furnished basins for numbers of small lakes. . . ." Forests, meadows, and waters clearly had not been superimposed on a "vast cinder" overnight. Doane was "profoundly impressed" with the landscape's "future importance to science, in unraveling mysteries hitherto unsolvable."

During the national park's first century, geology lacked a unifying idea as to what causes cycles of continuance and change, but one emerged in the 1960s. Geologists began to think change occurs as heat convection currents in the Earth's lower mantle push a mosaic of brittle plates across the planetary surface. As these plates interact, so geologists believe, enormous stress twists and cracks the Earth's crustal rocks. This pressure forces thick strata upward as mountain ranges and vents magma to the surface as volcanoes.

In the past 25 years this idea has been the basis of the well accepted theory called "plate tectonics," but, unfortunately, the driving force of tectonics cannot be directly observed. Evidence that crustal plates move across the surface abounds, but nobody has been 2,000 miles underground to confirm that the heat driving the plates comes from the Earth's mantle. It is unlikely anybody ever will, less likely, in fact, than that we should land humans on Mars.

Our home planet's paradoxical inaccessibility gives places like Yellowstone their extraordinary value. Such places provide the best "windows of information" we have. With its geothermal activity and lava flows, the park is a kind of messenger from inner space.

For all its great grandeur Yellowstone actually is a young place. It is younger than we are. Its present landscape came into existence long after the genus *Homo* developed in Africa.

Sedimentary rocks studded with fossil trilobites and other marine creatures in the park's peripheral peaks show that oceans covered Yellowstone's place on Earth for much of the past 400 million years. The sea finally receded near the end of the Dinosaur Age about 65 million years ago, a process recorded in Mount Everts, the sparsely vegetated ridge east of Mammoth Hot Springs.

Most of Mount Everts' sedimentary strata are whitish marine deposits. Recently, paleontologists found the bones of a plesiosaur, a giant marine reptile, and fossil clams in this area. Toward the top of the marine deposits, however, the strata become darker, more coarse, and thinner. These materials were deposited in a swampy river delta and have yielded fossil fragments of dinosaur eggs and plants that grew in fresh water, not sea water.

Yellowstone then lay at the western edge of North America. There a tectonic process called "subduction" was both destroying and creating new land as the crustal plate underlying the continent collided with the plate under the Pacific. Oceanic plates are composed of dark, heavy basaltic rocks similar to materials in the Earth's mantle, whereas continents largely are made up of lighter granitic rocks formed near the Earth's surface. The North American plate thus rode up over the denser Pacific plate, forcing it down into the Earth's mantle. Subduction's enormous stress and the high temperatures at such depth melted the sinking crustal plate into magma. The magma then rose back to the surface and formed volcanoes like those in today's Cascade Range in the Pacific Northwest—mounts St. Helens, Rainier, Shasta, and Baker.

Ancient volcanoes at Yellowstone erupted such vast amounts of ash that they covered entire subtropical and temperate forests that flourished in the warm valleys beneath them. The buried trees were fossilized, and erosion since has exposed some of them. Today, petrified trunks of redwoods like California's living trees still stand on cliffs overlooking the Lamar Valley. Their stony roots remain anchored in the 50-million-year-old substrate.

Other fossil trees include breadfruit, avocado, dogwood, sycamore, and hickory, all of which gradually vanished from the region as subduction kept building new land on North America's western margin and Yellowstone rose in elevation. The climate cooled and dried. By 20 million years ago pine forests replaced the redwoods.

We now know from fossils found elsewhere that such gradual change occurred, but little of this later geological record remains evident in the park. Catastrophic events that formed today's strange landscape destroyed most of the record. Drawing on tec-

Fire opens up lodgepole pine forests, allowing wildflowers such as the yellow heartleaf arnica and magenta fireweed to thrive.

When snow is on the ground, watch for moisture-loving and early-blooming flowers such as yellowbells.

tonic theory to understand these events, geologists theorize that a gigantic plume of molten matter emerged from the Earth's mantle below North America about 30 million years ago and rose toward the surface. The plume ascended slowly through the semi-plastic mantle, perhaps six inches a year, but by 15 million years ago it had neared the crust, becoming what is called a "hot spot."

Some 40 such hot spots exist on the planet. Their effects are dramatic. They can cause the Earth's crust to swell into blister-like domes, giant volcanoes that eventually explode and collapse, forming "calderas," giant bowl-shaped holes. The "vast cinder" of the Yellowstone Plateau is a caldera.

Geologists believe this hot spot left a track of calderas across the West's Great Basin after it surfaced, although it was not the hot spot that moved. What moved, and still moves, is the North American Plate. It is drifting, southwest, a few millimeters a year. Its track, so to speak, extends from northeastern Nevada across southern Idaho. It includes the remains of successively younger calderas.

By 2 million years ago the hot spot was in the Yellowstone region and apparently caused a volcanic explosion that dwarfs any recent ones. This stupendous explosion ejected 2,400 times more ash than Mount St. Helens's 1980 blast. The crater it left, Huckleberry Ridge Caldera, extended nearly 50 miles, from Yellowstone's center to Idaho's Island Park. Another explosion about 1.3 million years ago ejected more ash than Tambora, the volcano on Indonesia's Sumbawa island, which, in 1815, produced the biggest volcanic explosion ever recorded.

Yet another eruption 630,000 years ago—it blasted out the present-day Yellowstone Caldera and rivaled the blast creating the Huckleberry Ridge Caldera—defines today's Yellowstone Plateau. One can see this well from atop Mount Washburn on the caldera's northern rim. To the south over the meadows of Hayden Valley and the expanse of Yellowstone Lake is a line of peaks, the Red Mountains, the highest being Mount Sheridan. The line of peaks marks the caldera's southern rim. All the vast landscape between those distant peaks and Mount Washburn was part of the ancient volcanic range that exploded and collapsed, perhaps in mere hours. Having blasted away whatever geological deposits had existed above it, the hot spot shaped the strange landscape we know. Its heat and uplift cracked the rocks with many faults, creating steep escarpments like Mount Everts. Within the Lava Creek Caldera, where molten magma remains as close as three miles below the surface, lava emerged from fault lines and accumulated as the massive surface flows that now fill the caldera and the plateau's valleys. Formed of a volcanic material known as rhyolite, this lava was stiffer than basaltic lava and accumulated in "piles of taffy-like incandescent rock," as geologists have described it. Between the lava flows, thermal fields developed as groundwater drained into the heated bedrock and erupted back to the surface as hot springs or geysers. The hot springs and geysers deposited dissolved minerals in the fantastic shapes we see today. Yellowstone contains more than 300 geysers—approximately two-thirds of the planet's entire stock of geysers—and there are some 10,000 thermal features in all.

Even before the Lava Creek explosion, however, another shaping force had struck Yellowstone. About 1.5 million years ago, global climate changed and temperatures dropped lower than they had in hundreds of millions of years. At higher latitudes and altitudes winter snow no longer melted in summer but accumulated into glaciers, compressed ice that became plastic and flowed.

The Yellowstone Plateau is 8,000 feet above sea level. Ice covered it at least 10 times as climate fluctuated through the Pleistocene epoch. The latest, the Pinedale glaciation, covered the plateau with ice almost a mile thick from 80,000 to 15,000 years ago. One could have walked across the Pinedale ice and seen no more of Yellowstone than a few mountaintops. Ice covered even Mount Washburn—witness the glacial "polish" on its summit. The area of the Grand Canyon of the Yellowstone is also littered with granite boulders the glaciers dragged from the Beartooth Mountains north of the park.

One of the strangest things about Yellowstone's past is that thermal activity continued beneath these mammoth glaciers. Yellowstone's thermal works melted parts of the massive ice sheets to form caves where streams flowed into lakes. Traces of this melting are scattered about the park in the shape of kames, hills formed in thermal fields when the ice

dropped the rocks and sand it had picked up as it flowed. Among the biggest kames, Twin Buttes, west of the Midway Geyser Basin, may have accumulated suddenly when a lake beneath the glacier broke its dam. An abrupt change in pressure as the water rushed away may have produced a gigantic steam explosion that instantly melted the overlying ice and brought down an avalanche of debris. Steam still rises from this kame's top, and one of the Firehole Valley's oldest active geysers lies at its foot.

Common in Yellowstone, the coyote is often mistaken for the much larger wolf. Its huge ears help the coyote locate voles and mice beneath the snow.

The Pinedale glaciation left a veneer of glacial-till plains and lakes on the Yellowstone Plateau. Yellowstone Lake is the largest high-altitude lake in North America: its surface covers 136 square miles, and it is more than 400 feet deep. It still seems close to its glacial origins: its average summer temperature is 45°F, and it freezes three feet deep each winter except for a few spots like West Thumb where hot springs border it. Thermal vents also occur in the lake's depths and have created a strange underwater realm scientists are just beginning to explore.

In the 15,000 years after the glaciers melted, running water put the last touches on today's Yellowstone. It dissected marshy plains and converted the clay beds of former lakes into meadows like those of Hayden and Lamar valleys. The Yellowstone River rapidly cut its Grand Canyon, and now drops over the unaltered lava flows that form its falls and into thick strata of rhyolitic rock softened by ancient thermal fields. From Artist Point the canyon now looks like a gigantic trench dug in one of today's thermal fields.

Of course, Yellowstone wasn't finished when the Lava Creek volcano exploded or the Pinedale glaciers melted. Glaciation may well return someday, and a geothermal plume can exist 100 million years, judging from the ages of other hot spots. "Resurgent domes" like the Mallard Lake Dome near Old Faithful continue to rise as molten material expands beneath the surface, and earthquakes can and do change thermal fields overnight. They choke some hot springs and open others. But volcanism and climate aren't the only forces of change shaping Yellowstone. A new, living force entered the region soon after the Pinedale glaciers disappeared. In some ways this new force would have a greater effect than a million years of eruptions and ice caps.

For geysers to occur there must be heat, water, and a plumbing system (see detail at right). A magma chamber, shown below, provides the heat, which radiates into surrounding rock. Water from rain and snow works its way underground through fractures in the rock. As the water reaches hot rock it begins to rise back to the surface, passing through the rock rhyolite, which is former volcanic ash or lava rich in silica. The hot water dissolves the silica and carries it upward to line rock crevices. This forms a constriction that holds in the mounting pressure, creating a geyser's plumbing system.

As superheated water nears the surface, its pressure drops, and the water flashes into steam as a geyser. Hot springs have unconstricted plumbing systems. Fumaroles (steam vents) do, too, but are generally dry. Mud-

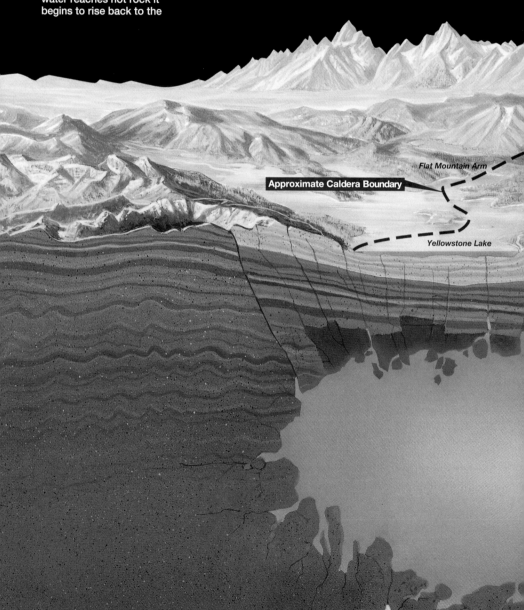

Flat Mountain Arm

Approximate Caldera Boundary

Yellowstone Lake

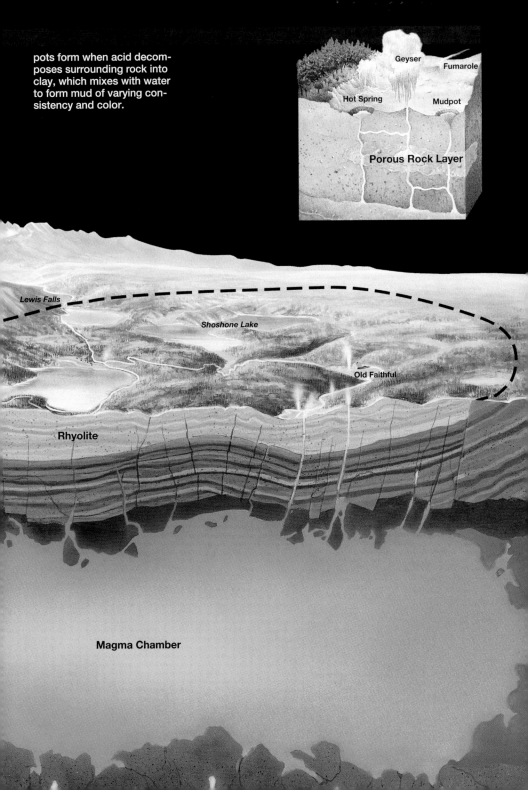

...pots form when acid decomposes surrounding rock into clay, which mixes with water to form mud of varying consistency and color.

Geyser

Fumarole

Hot Spring

Mudpot

Porous Rock Layer

Lewis Falls

Shoshone Lake

Old Faithful

Rhyolite

Magma Chamber

Yellowstone's Volcanic Caldera

An erupting volcano may expel so much magma that the roof of its emptied magma chamber collapses. The resulting depression is called a caldera—Spanish for cauldron. That happened here 630,000 years ago, and the black line on the painting (looking due South) locates the rim of Yellowstone's caldera. Later lava flows filled in much of the caldera, but it was originally 45 miles long, 30 miles wide, and up to thousands of feet deep. You can see its rim from several areas in the park, including Mount Washburn, Gibbon Falls, Lewis Falls, and Yellowstone Lake's Flat Mountain Arm. Today's

Flat Mountain Arm

Yellowstone Lake

Mount Washburn

caldera is not the area's first caldera. Powerful volcanic forces had erupted here 2 million years ago and again 1.3 million years ago. Three calderas progress, oldest to youngest, from beyond the southwest park boundary to the center of the park. Their positions track how the North American crustal plate has moved over a stationary hot spot—picture passing a sheet of paper over a fixed candle flame. The event 2 million years ago is considered the largest volcanic eruption ever on Earth. The eruption 630,000 years ago was much smaller but still 1,000 times more powerful than the Mount St. Helens explosion in 1980. If major volcanic events occurred approximately every 600,000 years, with the most recent occurring more than 600,000 years ago, is another eruption due soon? No one can say. What is certain is that Yellowstone's scenery originates in its volcanic past.

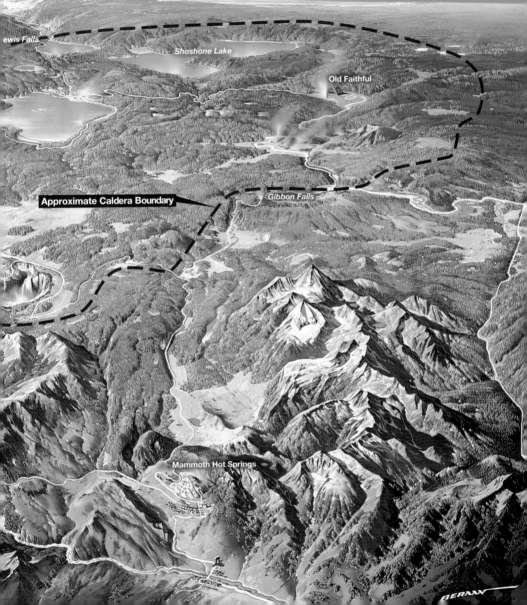

ewis Falls

Shoshone Lake

Old Faithful

Approximate Caldera Boundary

Gibbon Falls

Mammoth Hot Springs

BERANN

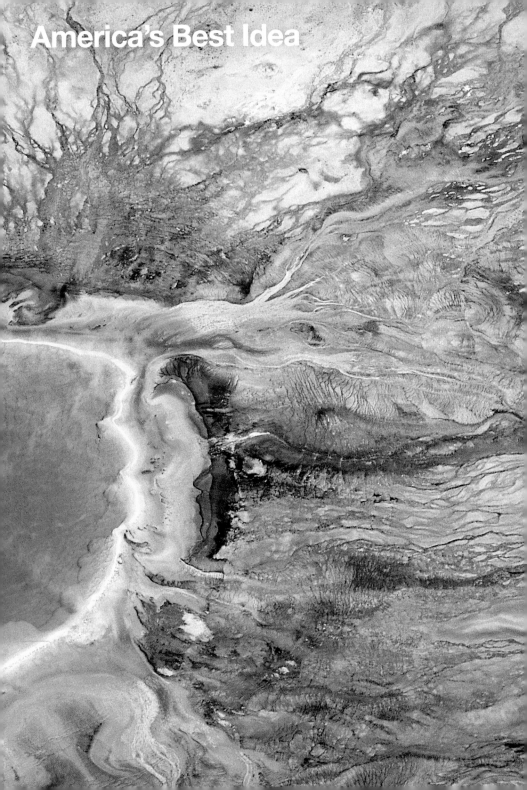

Part 2

America's Best Idea

Special, Sacred, And Wild Still

As I walked around one of the park's less-visited hot springs one day, I came upon a small cairn. Beside this pile of stones was a peeled stick wrapped in rawhide and decorated with feathers and a disk of green stone. I don't know what the significance of the little shrine was, or who made it, but I felt I was seeing something ancient, even though the stick and rawhide were new. I left it undisturbed, as I would have left undisturbed one of the 19th-century wickiups that still exist in the park—or any other cultural resource or artifact.

Early accounts of Native American visitors to Yellowstone mention them leaving offerings at thermal features to show reverence. Native Americans are reticent about such traditions, and there is little to document them. Nevertheless, it seems that Yellowstone generally has been regarded as a special or sacred place by the various cultures who have lived around it in historical times. If so, it probably was similarly regarded by the many generations who came before them. I may have been seeing an expression of one of Earth's oldest religions beside that hot spring.

Artifacts found near the park show that humans had entered the Yellowstone region as early as 11,500 years ago. A people called the "Clovis culture" made the earliest artifacts, which included stone projectile points used to kill large mammals. One such weapon—found near the park's north boundary—was made of obsidian, a glassy stone common in lava flows. One of North America's largest deposits of this stone is Obsidian Cliff in the park, so the point may have been quarried there. Slightly younger points from south of the park definitely were. Such hunting cultures surely crisscrossed Yellowstone many times in pursuit of game and must have known its strange landscape.

The region's rugged terrain and harsh winters probably made it harder to live in than the sur-

Petrified trees and other remains, such as leaves, seeds, and pollen, are direct evidence of the diverse forest ecosystems in Yellowstone's past. These forests were fossilized 45 to 55 million years ago after being covered with volcanic ash, which aided the preservation process.

rounding plains, yet considerable evidence of later prehistoric occupation exists. Surprisingly, funeral mounds of civilizations living in the Midwest 2,500 to 1,200 years ago have yielded ceremonial artifacts of stone from Yellowstone's Obsidian Cliff. A well-established trade network apparently extended throughout great portions of North America for more than a thousand years. We know less about the people who quarried Obsidian Cliff. For example, did they live on the plateau? Or did they just visit it to collect obsidian? About 1,500 years ago human population in this region seems to have begun increasing, judging from a number of sites around Yellowstone Lake and in the park's northern valleys. Arrowheads and pottery from these sites show that these important technological innovations had reached the region.

Native Americans known to have inhabited Yellowstone in historical times may have arrived 2,000 years ago, moving east from the Great Basin. When Europeans entered the region in the early 19th century, the Plains Shoshones had a horse-mounted, bison-hunting culture. The Yellowstone bands lived more simply, however, in keeping with the rocky, forested terrain. They hunted big game on foot, sometimes driving herds into corral traps made of tree trunks. Plains Shoshones called them "Sheep-eaters." Their favored game was bighorns, whose meat was generally esteemed. In 1835 the trapper Osborne Russell met a Sheepeater band in Lamar Valley. He described them as "neatly clothed in dressed deer and sheepskins of the best quality" and "well armed with bows and arrows pointed with obsidian." Eager to trade for metal utensils, the Sheepeaters told Russell that they could get "plenty of skins" but that they seldom met traders.

Other Native American groups have visited the Yellowstone Plateau in historic times. The Crows who lived east of it and the Blackfeet from the north traveled through on hunting, trading, or war-making trips. The Blackfeet sometimes fought with white trappers over beaver and other furbearers whose pelts were the early 19th-century West's most marketable resources. Joe Meek encountered the geyser field that he likened to industrial Pittsburgh while he was wandering through the area after a fight with Blackfeet in which two of his companions had been killed. By 1840 bison had vanished from the Snake River Plain. This forced a tribe called the Bannocks, who were related to the Paiutes farther south, to traverse the plateau yearly to and from summer bison hunting on the Great Plains. The Bannocks' trail parallels some of the park road, or vice versa, from Mammoth to the Lamar Valley. Stretches of the trail can be seen today.

In 1877 the Nez Perce crossed the five-year-old park, fleeing the U.S. Army. Encroaching settlers had displaced the originally friendly Nez Perce from their eastern Washington homeland. Some 750 Nez Perce wanted to join Sitting Bull in Canada instead of moving to a U.S. reservation. Sitting Bull was the principal architect of the coalition that defeated Colonel George Armstrong Custer at the Little Bighorn the year before. The Nez Perce crossed the center of the park along the creek named for them. They reached the Great Plains via the Lamar Valley and Clarks Fork Canyon. The Nez Perce got within 40 miles of Canada before the Army stopped them in a six-day battle, leading Chief Joseph to declare: "From where the sun now stands I will fight no more forever."

Angry at the deaths of some women and children in an earlier fight at Montana's Big Hole River, Nez Perce warriors took hostage or attacked several tourist parties in Yellowstone and raided Mammoth Hot Springs. They shot one irascible tourist named George Cowan in the head and leg and left him for dead. Cowan regained consciousness, however, and started hobbling toward his camp, whereupon he was shot again in the hip. After also surviving accidental near-drowning and burns, Cowan reached safety at last. Army surgeons found the bullet that had knocked him out protruding from his forehead. Cowan complained that the surgeons were more interested in the geysers than his wounds, but he recovered.

According to their tourist hostages, the fleeing Nez Perce stopped to have a look at the geysers just like other travelers. A Nez Perce named Yellow Wolf later said they'd known about Yellowstone and its hot springs before 1877. This contradicts the legend that Native Americans were superstitiously afraid of the thermal features, an impression today's historians think resulted from a misinterpretation of

Bison: Native Mainstay and Cultural Symbol

When Congress named Yellowstone a national park in 1872, many Americans were already alarmed at the rapid disappearance of wildlife in the United States. Bison (*Bison bison*) had been the economic mainstay of various Plains tribes, who used the entire animal: horns, brain, skull, hair, hide, meat, fat, tongue, and dung. The tails were used as tipi ornaments or fly brushes. At one time bison ranged from Canada to Georgia. Some estimates put their population in the early 1800s at 30 to 60 million. But by 1832 there were no more bison east of the Mississippi River, and by the 1870s bison seemed fated to vanish west of it, too. Market hunters shot bison for their hides or sometimes just the tongues. Sport hunters fired blindly at herds from passing trains. After the Civil War, as herds dwindled and pressure mounted to move the Plains tribes onto reservations, the Army drove away or killed herds. Yellowstone's bison have survived in the wild since prehistoric time—but poaching nearly eliminated them shortly after 1900. The bison population here today comes from two bloodlines: the original wild group and the bison introduced in 1902. The bison, often called "buf-

falo," has become an American cultural symbol that has adorned a nickel, postage stamps, and the U.S. Department of the Interior seal and National Park Service logo. At right is a European artist's conception of the American bison in the 1550s. *Buffalo Hunt*—the large painting—is by Arthur F. Tait, a 19th-century artist.

Expeditions and Surveys

When the nation turned its energy to the West after the Civil War, tales of Yellowstone's thermal features quickly inspired people to investigate. Native Americans, trappers, and miners knew the Yellowstone country before expeditions began exploring it. Reports of its wonders moved Congress to fund a scientific exploration of Yellowstone in 1871 by the Hayden Expedition, with a simultaneous survey by the U.S. Army Corps of Engineers. With expeditions elsewhere led by Clarence King, John Wesley Powell, and Lt. George Montague Wheeler, the 1871 Hayden Expedition was one of the four great surveys of the West. It was led by Dr. Ferdinand V. Hayden, a physician turned geologist, explorer, naturalist, and influential publicist of the West's scientific wonders, scenic beauty, and economic potential. Money from Northern Pacific Railroad promoter Jay Cooke enabled Hayden to take along photographer William Henry Jackson, sketch-artists Henry W. Elliot and W.H. Holmes, and painter Thomas Moran. Their compelling visual proof for the expedition reports sparked national interest in Yellowstone. Hayden, other explorers, and the railroad lobbied Congress to save the area from private development.

This mule-drawn odometer (below) measured distances for the 1871 Hayden Survey map (background image) of the Yellowstone country and environs.

Members of Hayden's 1872 expedition, left to right, are: W.H. Holmes, artist; unidentified; Frank H. Bradley, geologist; W.H. Jackson, photographer; L.R. Campbell, Jackson's assistant; and Dr. A.C. Peale, mineralogist.

Based on its 1864 precedent of granting public domain lands in Yosemite Valley to California for parkland, Congress set aside Yellowstone as the nation's first national park. President Ulysses S. Grant signed the legislation into law on March 1, 1872. The expedition's boat *Anna* is shown at left on Yellowstone Lake. Jackson, the photographer, later mislabeled it "Annie."

A.D. Wilson (right) sights a transit on Hayden's 1874 survey of Colorado. Hayden used a transit like the one below. In the background is Hayden's field notebook of the 1871 expedition.

the Native Americans' respectful attitude. Elsewhere, trappers and explorers often met them near thermal fields and described them bathing and cooking in hot springs, neither of which suggests a fearful response.

Each native culture and even individuals regarded Yellowstone differently, of course. The Shoshones and Bannocks apparently had a more religious attitude toward this area than the Blackfeet, whose own main sacred sites lay farther north. Some Native Americans also exempted whites from attack if they seemed touched by the spirits. They allegedly called geologist Ferdinand Hayden "Picks-up-stones-running" and let him roam the Great Plains unmolested collecting rocks and fossils.

Trappers like Osborne Russell were the first people other than Native Americans known to enter the Yellowstone region. The Lewis and Clark Expedition of 1804-1806 passed north of what is now the park, but one of its members, John Colter, crossed it during a trapping foray in 1807-1808. Colter apparently saw thermal features near Tower Fall. In the ensuing half-century, several such travelers also visited the region and left descriptions like Joe Meek's of thermal areas. Meek may have seen the Norris Geyser Basin. He later reported that he was ascending a "low mountain" from which "the whole country beyond was smoking with the vapor from boiling springs, and burning with gasses, issuing from small craters, each of which was emitting a sharp, whistling sound." It was "the rising smoke and vapor" of that frosty morning that reminded him of Pittsburgh. Meek apparently got carried away with his story at that point, because he next describes craters "from four to six miles across" out of which "issued blue flames and molten brimstone." Such wonders simply don't exist, not even in Yellowstone. At least not yet.

As in prehistoric times, Yellowstone's ruggedness and hard winters probably made it less visited even by mountain men than other parts of the West. This isolation only encouraged exaggerations like Meek's and those attributed to fur trader Jim Bridger, who raised the "tall tale" to an art form. Bridger worked stories from disparate origins into his repertoire for entertaining the parties of settlers and soldiers he guided. One tale concerned a "glass mountain" so transparent Bridger tried to shoot an elk through it. Another told not only of petrified trees but petrified birds singing petrified songs. Bridger evidently had stock petrification stories, but the locale was indefinite. Such stories didn't make Yellowstone much better known. News media tended to ignore them. Most Americans considered Yellowstone itself a tall tale through the 1850s. Even when its existence was confirmed, people mostly kept calling it "Wonderland"—as though still not convinced of its reality despite the evidence.

Yellowstone's isolation from the United States began to dissolve in the 1860s as gold strikes in the Montana and Idaho territories drew prospectors into the area. Had a significant Yellowstone strike occurred, national park history certainly would have been quite different. As it was, the thermal fields and other features became well known enough that a Wyoming newspaper, the *Frontier Index*, predicted in 1867: "A few years more and the Union Pacific Railroad will bring thousands of pleasure seekers, sight seers, and invalids from every part of the globe to see this land of surpassing wonders." Even the *Index* fed the tradition of exaggerating its wonders. In an 1869 article it said Yellowstone Lake was "filled with the fish half as large as a man, some of which have a mouth and horns and skin like a catfish and legs like a lizard."

In 1869 three young men who would liken mudpots to "chemical works" made a 36-day horseback tour from Montana, traversing the Yellowstone River watershed upstream to Yellowstone Lake, then returning via the Firehole and Madison rivers. The three men were tourists: they came to explore Yellowstone for its own sake. Two of them, David Folsom and Charles Cook, collaborated on an article that appeared in the July 1870 *Western Monthly* after other periodicals rejected it, calling it "unreliable." Those rejections weren't fair: their account was authentic, especially compared to what had come before. Yet one can't altogether blame unreceptive editors who might find descriptions like the following on their desks: "In some springs the water was clear and transparent; others contained so much sulphur that they looked like pots of boiling yellow paint. One of the largest was as black as ink. . . . At the bottom of the slope was a vat, ten by thirty feet,

Continued on page 54

47

Yellowstone by Railroad and Coach

Jay Cooke and the Northern Pacific Railroad sought to have Yellowstone made a national park so they could profit from it without owning it. Cooke failed to profit from it because of the depression of 1873. Ten years later a reorganized Northern Pacific Railroad completed its line across Montana and a spur track south to Yellowstone from Livingston. Enjoying a virtual monopoly on access to the park, the railroad went all-out promoting it and realizing its tourist potential. The railroad began a guidebook series in 1883 with *The Yellowstone National Park*. By 1886 it was underwriting construction of hotels that were a day's journey apart by horse-drawn coach and near the major park attractions. (It took about five horse-drawn days to see the park, and the railroad also owned a stagecoach concession.) Stages later met visitors at the Gardiner train station once the Northern Pacific had extended its spur track almost up to the park entrance. Stages then pulled visitors through the memorial arch (right). In 1915 the railroads brought in 44,477 of the park's 51,895 visitors; cars brought in only 7,418. By 1930 only 26,845 of the year's 194,771 visitors came

by rail. In 1917 caravans of concessioner touring buses had begun carrying visitors through the park. Later concessioner fleets of bigger park buses (below, right) took visitors touring. The railroad defended the new park and later advocated enlarging it to protect ranging wildlife. The National Hotel (large photo) was the first hotel built at Mammoth Hot Springs, in 1883.

Fort Yellowstone: The Army Takes Charge

Congress created Yellowstone National Park but gave no direction—or money—on how to run or protect it. Decades of trial and error went into deciding how to administer and protect this new thing, a national park. Meanwhile, poachers, squatters, and vandals created huge problems. "What has the Government done," a Montana newspaper asked in 1874, "to render this national elephant approachable and attractive since its adoption as one of the nation's pets? Nothing." A string of superintendents with no pay (at first) and no enforcement power met with mixed or no success. Finally, the Secretary of the Interior asked the U.S. Army for temporary help. Fifty men of Company M, First United States Cavalry, marched to Mammoth Hot Springs from Fort Custer in Montana Territory, arriving August 17, 1886. In fact the Army would stay 32 years—and play an important role in the history of Yellowstone. The Army helped shape the later National Park Service, its ranger ethic, and its policies for protecting natural parks. While in Yellowstone the Army built many facilities: Fort Yellowstone (started in 1891), soldier stations, and backcountry cabins, many still used today. Fort Yellowstone at Mammoth Hot Springs consists of 35 military structures from the 1890s and early 1900s, and it looks like the military acad-

emy at West Point, New York. The Army stayed on in the park for two years after Congress created the National Park Service in 1916, and, even after the Army left, some soldiers remained and became civilian park rangers. The large photo shows Fort Yellowstone in 1903. The men at right were on winter patrol.

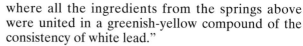

where all the ingredients from the springs above were united in a greenish-yellow compound of the consistency of white lead."

Although not widely read, the so-called Folsom account helped motivate a much larger expedition led by Henry Washburn, surveyor general of Montana. The Washburn expedition explored the park along a similar route in September 1870 and produced several published accounts, including the one by Lieutenant Doane that likened the plateau to a "vast cinder." Articles by Nathaniel Langford and Truman Everts in *Scribner's Monthly* for the summer and fall of 1871 received particular attention, not least because Everts got lost on the expedition. He wandered alone for 37 days, hallucinating and living on "one snow bird, two small minnows" and thistle roots.

Prospector Jack Baronet, who finally rescued Everts, at first mistook him for a bear and prepared to shoot him. Then Baronet noticed "it was making a low groaning noise, crawling along upon its knees and elbows. . . . Then it suddenly occurred to me that it was the object of my search."

Geologist Ferdinand Hayden led a government-sponsored expedition in 1871. And the Hayden expedition returned not only with written descriptions but with a compellingly vivid visual record created by photographer William Henry Jackson and painter Thomas Moran .

So many expeditions filing in and out have raised a question: who first thought of making Yellowstone a park? Historian Aubrey Haines wrote that Montana territorial governor Thomas F. Meagher suggested it in 1865 and that David Folsom also did after his 1869 expedition. Legends tend to grow up around seminal ideas, however. According to a popular story, the Washburn party had a momentous discussion while camped at the confluence of the Firehole and Gibbon rivers in September 1870. "It was suggested that it would be a 'profitable speculation' to take up land around the various objects of interest," wrote Hiram Chittenden, the early park historian. "The conversation had not proceeded far on these lines when one of the party, Cornelius Hedges, interposed and said that private ownership of that region, or any part of it, ought never to be countenanced; but that it ought to be set apart by the government and forever held to the unrestricted use of the people. This higher view of the subject found immediate acceptance with the other members of the party." This dramatic story became the "authorized version" of the park initiative. At the site, a bronze plaque's bas-relief shows a messianic Hedges fascinating a campfire group with his vision.

Research into the Washburn party journals yields no conclusive evidence that such a drama ever occurred. Today it is considered a colorful legend, one of many that continue to resonate despite the facts. However, with a broad meadow stretching to the river and the fluted lava cliffs of National Park Mountain in the background, their campsite near today's Madison Junction does seem to epitomize Yellowstone's scenery.

To be sure, not all supporters of the park were without financial self-interest. The management of the Northern Pacific Railroad, and Montana's business community in general, expected to profit as tourists swept in "from every part of the globe." The railroad funded Langford to travel to Washington and lobby for the park. Yet genuine enthusiasm went into the park bill, too. Ferdinand Hayden developed an exhibition of photographs and geological specimens that helped to convince the public and legislators of Yellowstone's value. The campaign worked: the bill was submitted to Congress in January 1872, and the legislation was signed into law by President Ulysses S. Grant on March 1.

In one sense history came to an unprecedented end when the park was established and Native American occupation of the park gradually diminished, then ended. Of course, people kept visiting Yellowstone, many more than in the past. Yet, aside from rare episodes like the Nez Perce War, something new subordinated the desires and fears that usually drive history. Yellowstone became a place not so much for human actions as for the contemplation of them. Perhaps Yellowstone had always been such a place for Native Americans, but for western civilization this was a new, or at least a rediscovered, idea. There had been places for contemplation, of course, churches and universities, but never before a whole region the size of a state or principality. This is not to say the park embalmed the history preceding it. This may seem the case in

Old Faithful Inn

"More than any other building in the national parks," wrote architectural historian Harvey H. Kaiser, "the Old Faithful Inn not only met but far exceeded the concessioner's ideas for development." Yellowstone Park Association, a concessioner whose silent partner was the Northern Pacific Railroad, hired 29-year-old Seattle architect Robert C. Reamer in 1902 to design an inn at Old Faithful Geyser. It was built in 1903 and 1904 with local stone and timber in the rustic style for $140,000 plus $25,000 for furnishings. Its seven-story, log-framed lobby soars 91 feet to the roofline. "The lobby was the focus of Mr. Reamer's rustic effect," historian Aubrey L. Haines wrote. "It is a great, balconied cavern, open to the roof, with all supporting beams and braces exposed to view like the skeleton of some enormous mammal seen from within." You must stand on more than one of its balconies to grasp this spectacle. The wrought-iron work was largely forged on site. The inn's chalet features applied to its log skeleton typify the rustic style. The inn was meant to blunt

competition from rival Union Pacific Railroad packaged tours that came in Yellowstone's West Entrance. The east wing was added in 1913 and 1914; the west wing in 1927. These people watched Old Faithful erupt in 1905 (small photo), a year after the original inn was finished.

the more heavily used areas. In such areas Yellowstone can appear to be an outdoor museum indeed, but that is merely a veneer. Only yards away from most of the park's roads and trailheads one quickly confronts a landscape that has changed very little from the world the mountain men and Sheepeaters knew so intimately.

I remember driving up the little spur to Sheepeater Cliff south of Mammoth Hot Springs late one autumn afternoon. It is a sheltered gorge where the people whose name was given to the cliff faced the morning sun and the clear water of the Gardner River, backed with fragrant aspen groves. Although I was only a few feet from my car, in that place their life seemed more immediate than the bustle of life at the park hotels and visitor centers. Theirs was a life almost unimaginably strenuous to us, but it was also familiar to us—in the beauty and diversity that surrounded it.

This wickiup or shelter represents evidence of human activity, which dates back more than 10,000 years here.

Opposite: *The identity of this family, photographed south of Yellowstone, is not known. Many different Native Americans have lived in or traveled through the Yellowstone area. More than 20 tribes have declared varying degrees of historical association with this special place.*

Protecting Nature

The surest way to experience Yellowstone's continuity with its past is to encounter its wildlife. Seeing an elk, bison, or moose in the forests and meadows is really not so different from seeing a mammoth—all recall the shaggy world of the ice ages. There's something wonderfully monstrous about them, too. This monstrousness may seem a bit ludicrous at park hotels, as rutting bull elks chase cows across the lawns with wheezy, discordant cries. Yet, out among the canyons, when migrating bluebirds flutter like chips of autumn sky in the aspen trees, these same high-pitched cries sound very different. They echo and reverberate powerfully, thoroughly justifying the impressive term—"bugling"—which is used to describe them.

Life returned quickly to Yellowstone after the Pinedale glaciers melted. Scientists can reconstruct how plants did so by identifying and dating pollen in glacial pond mud. The earliest vegetation was low-growing tundra like that still covering Mount Washburn and other summits. Trees soon followed, since they'd been growing in adjacent, ice-free areas throughout the episode of glaciation. Engelmann spruce was the first, about 13,200 years ago, which suggests that the climate was cool and wet then. After another 500 years whitebark and lodgepole pine appeared, probably a result of warmer, drier conditions.

Lodgepole remains the predominant tree on the infertile rhyolite soils of Yellowstone's caldera, although spruce and subalpine fir replace it eventually, if the forest is not burned. The Douglas fir and aspen found at lower elevations of the park's north end moved in by 10,000 years ago. Some of the aspens may be the original plants—as we know now from their genetic fingerprints. An aspen can reproduce indefinitely as a "clone," a colony of roots and stems genetically the same as one seed that germinated long ago.

Climate sets strict limits on Yellowstone's flora, but wildflowers growing in sunny places during the short summer can be extravagant. When I camped in the backcountry, it was impossible to put up a tent without crushing some of the magenta paintbrush, yellow composites, blue lupine, and pink elephanthead that covered the open slopes in every direction. This was in mid-August. When I got up the next morning I thought summer was suddenly over. Every flower was white and drooping with frost. Yet within an hour after sunlight reached them, they were as lush as in the previous afternoon. Maybe these flowers' hardiness developed during the ice ages.

Animals followed the plants, and Yellowstone's "megafauna" 12,000 years ago must have included the extinct wooly mammoths, saber-tooth cats, and ground sloths, although their fossils have yet to be found in the park. Fossils found recently in a small cave in Lamar Valley show that the fauna throughout the past 2,000 years has been very like today's. Bushy-tailed woodrats or "packrats" living in the cave collected bits of bone from the surroundings, as is the species' strange habit, and deposited them in their nests. In those ancient middens researchers have found the bones of elk, bison, pronghorns, bighorns, coyotes, wolves, foxes, beavers, and grizzly bears, as well as smaller species such as marmots, squirrels, rabbits, skunks, bats, mice, and even fish.

Next to scenery and geological wonders, Yellowstone's wildlife has been the park's greatest attraction, yet this biological resource has proved both harder to understand and more difficult to conserve than geysers and waterfalls. Public attitudes toward wild creatures have undergone profound changes, and wildlife management policies sometimes have been reversed. In fact, many questions still remain as to how park animals relate to their environment, to each other, and to human use of the park.

In the mid-19th century many Americans still relied partly on wildlife for food. This reliance, combined with wasteful slaughter for hides or sport, was decimating wildlife throughout North America by the 1870s. Early conservationists saw Yellowstone as a refuge for the threatened species, and their vision would prove shockingly true over the next two decades. Bison, elk, pronghorns, bighorns, and even deer disappeared from vast areas where they had abounded, and it seemed entirely possible that big game would become extinct in this country. By the end of the 19th century, Yellowstone had the last free-roaming bison herd in the United States and one of the last elk herds, although the animals still weren't safe even in the park. Army Captain William Ludlow reported in 1875 that hide-hunters had killed as many as 2,000 elk within 15 miles of Mammoth Hot Springs that one winter alone. They left the skinned carcasses to rot.

In 1894 a single poacher operating with a powerful repeating rifle in the remote Pelican Valley might have exterminated the park's remaining bison if two U.S. cavalrymen hadn't apprehended him. A public outcry arising from this episode led within 13 days to Congress passing the Lacey Act, which provided, for the first time, federal penalties for the poaching of wildlife.

Yet persistent poaching in the park reduced bison to fewer than 50 animals by 1898. Park managers responded to this dire situation by doing everything in their power to protect grazing wildlife. When enforcement of the Lacey Act eventually reduced poaching pressure, the park's managers turned their attention to animal predators. They succeeded in extirpating wolves from the park by the 1930s.

After a 1902 survey showed only 23 remaining in the park, bison were managed more as domestic animals than wild ones. The Lamar Valley became a "bison ranch," complete with corrals, fences, and fields plowed to raise fodder. Under the direction of a flamboyant frontiersman called "Buffalo Jones," captive bison from Montana and Texas were raised with the native herd to increase numbers. Park managers also fed hay to elk, pronghorn, and deer in the valleys to prevent starvation during Yellowstone's harsh winters,

Early managers tried to domesticate other aspects of the park. Believing that wildfire threatened animals as well as visitors, they fought the lightning fires that once had burned unchecked. About 40 percent of park streams and lakes were naturally empty of native cutthroat trout, arctic grayling, or whitefish. So park managers stocked them, often with non-native species: rainbow, brown, lake, and brook trout. They built a hatchery to grow native

Next pages: For elk, autumn is the time to mate. This bull's large antlers communicate his dominance to cow elk and rival bulls. His bugling conveys the same message.

Continued on page 72

65

Natural-Process Management

Preserving national parks in the United States grew from the appreciation of scenery. Many 19th-century thinkers promoted the contemplation of majestic, sublime natural scenery for those positive emotional, psychological, intellectual, and health benefits it produced. As a result, the management of natural areas focused on protecting scenery against change, and what proponents of scenic preservation did not see was that some of the forces of change—such as fire—help maintain the dynamic natural conditions so visible in Yellowstone. Early 20th-century wildlife managers took their cue from livestock husbandry: wild species they deemed useful or desirable to humans would be better off, they reasoned, if their predators were eliminated. But such early wildlife managers had yet to learn about or appreciate a holistic, ecological viewpoint—the totality of relationships to other species and their environ-

1. Osprey
2. Coyote
3. Mule deer
4. Bighorn sheep
5. Gray wolf
6. Bull elk
7. Grizzly bear and cub
8. Bull moose
9. Uinta ground squirrel

ment. In the 1960s, national parks began to strive to maintain all the native components and processes of the naturally evolving landscape. These include the natural abundance, diversity, and ecological integrity of the plants and animals that evolved in each park—its biodiversity. In today's view,

natural change is integral to functioning natural systems. To minimize or reverse the unwanted effects of past management practices, like the stocking of non-native fish or the removal of natural predators, we sometimes must intervene to restore natural conditions—see Fire's Natural Role in Wildlands, page 76; Greater

Yellowstone Ecosystem, page 92; and Restoring Wolves, page 96. Effective natural-process management and restoration work require strong science programs, which can be funded only with public support.

10. Black bear
11. American white pelican
12. Yellow-bellied marmot
13. Pika
14. Bison and calf

15. Lesser scaup
16. Trumpeter swans
17. Green-winged teal
18. Pronghorn

Securing a Future for Grizzly Bears

Yellowstone retains one of the few wild populations of grizzly bears in the lower 48 States. The grizzly is a sub-species of the brown bear that entered North America from Asia 50,000 years ago. Plains tribes invoked this great bear's awesome spirit in dance and ceremony and hunted it, too. The grizzly symbolizes wildness. It is a magnificent predator at the top of the food chain. Grizzly bears are generally larger than black bears. Male grizzlies will average 400 to 600 pounds here, females 200 to 350 pounds. Both can sprint up to 35 or 40 miles per hour. Rearing up on its hind legs, an adult may stand more than eight feet tall. Since 1975 the grizzly has been protected as a threatened species under the Endangered Species Act. A grizzly bear requires great living space: a male in greater Yellowstone will range over 800 to 2,000 square miles; a female will range over 300 to 500 square miles. Park or

forest boundaries cannot contain the grizzly, and this has helped inspire multi-agency cooperation in protecting it throughout the Greater Yellowstone Ecosystem (see page 92). Logging, mining, increasing human population, more home building, and more recreation use threaten the bear's future. Reducing and fragmenting grizzly habitat results in more conflicts between bears and humans and livestock, and in more bears getting hit by vehicles. Roads and fragmented habitat also facilitate poaching. Exotic organisms introduced by humans, such as fish-eating lake trout, invasive weed plants, and blister-rust fungus on white pines, also threaten the grizzly's food supply. Because of their low reproduction rate, protection of breeding females is key to the grizzly bear's recovery. Scientists radio-collar bears, such as the one shown here, so they can monitor their location and behavior.

cutthroats and shipped the eggs and fry elsewhere. White pelicans eat fish, so park managers even went around the lake's pelican rookery crushing their eggs so there would be more trout for fishermen. In effect, they were trying to run Yellowstone almost as if it was a farm or a city park.

The park's big game began to seem secure by 1916 when the bison herd reached 348. Yet other worries arose. Elk numbers had increased rapidly, particularly in the park's fertile northern range, and the park's managers feared the elk would deplete their food supply and starve. They also feared the teeming elk might eat up the food of other animals, such as bighorn sheep or even beavers, which prefer the aspens and willows, which elk browse heavily.

So strong had these fears grown by the 1930s that the National Park Service began culling the elk herd. At first they shipped the "surplus" animals elsewhere. Later they shot the elk and gave the meat to Indian reservations. Still, elk numbers kept surging above the 5,000 to 7,000 then thought suitable for the northern range. By the 1960s the National Park Service was eliminating thousands of elk yearly, driving them into butchering pens with helicopters. The situation drew increasing media attention and public alarm.

Meanwhile, the scientific concern for wildlife generally had undergone a major shift in its focus. Now predators were endangered—the wolf was virtually extinct in the West by the 1950s—and situations like Yellowstone's elk "overpopulation" made biologists question whether managing wildlife like livestock was practical.

In 1963 an influential government committee that was chaired by University of California Professor A. Starker Leopold recommended that "the biotic associations within each park be maintained, or where necessary recreated, as nearly as possible in the condition that prevailed when the area was first visited by the white man." In keeping with this Leopold Report, as it came to be known, the National Park Service adopted a "natural regulation" wildlife policy. It discontinued artificial feeding and elk culling. (Bison ranching was discontinued by 1952, and fish hatcheries had been phased out by 1960.) It adopted a "natural burn" policy toward lightning fires in the backcountry. The reasoning: because the park's ecosystem has adapted to fire for millions of years, burning has a creative as well as a destructive role, returning dead plant nutrients to the soil and fostering new growth.

These policies are seen as ongoing experiments. Park managers are free to depart from them when, for example, animals or fires may threaten human safety. Despite this considerable flexibility, the policies still have drawn criticism.

"Yellowstone elk have been controversial nationally so often," Paul Schullery wrote in *Mountain Time*, a 1983 book about his experiences as a park naturalist, "that they have a greater and more avid constituency than many politicians."

Elk numbers have grown considerably from 1960s lows, and some people think there are too many, although the elk have yet to extirpate other species from the park. Nor have elk destroyed park grasslands. Many have dispersed into formerly unoccupied range north of the park. Bison also have increased until some have tried to migrate westward to lower-lying areas, causing conflicts with neighboring ranchers because some bison can carry brucellosis, also a disease of cattle.

The loudest and most strident controversy over the new policies concerned the wildfires in 1988, which affected nearly one third of the park. News media emphasized the fires' danger and destructiveness, and critics charged that the natural burn policy had let the fires get out of control. Yet then-Park Superintendent Robert Barbee had suspended the policy early in the summer, and many firefighters doubted the partly human-caused blazes could have been controlled any more than they were, given that year's unprecedentedly dry conditions and weather patterns.

"The problem was that no one had ever seen fire behavior like this before," the park's chief ranger said. "Fires that in any normal year would have petered out after a dozen acres were still raging hundreds of thousands of acres later."

Despite apocalyptic newscasts the fires did not damage Yellowstone ecologically. Vegetation began recovering quickly. Wildlife losses from fire or smoke inhalation were surprisingly light. Some 243 elk, five bison, two moose, and four deer were known to have died in the park, although more animals suc-

Next pages: *Fire in Yellowstone is as natural as rain and as necessary. Woodpeckers, bluebirds, and other cavity nesters make homes in dead trees. Elk digest tree bark more easily because fire burns off toxins. Fire also stimulates the growth of lodgepole pine and aspen.*

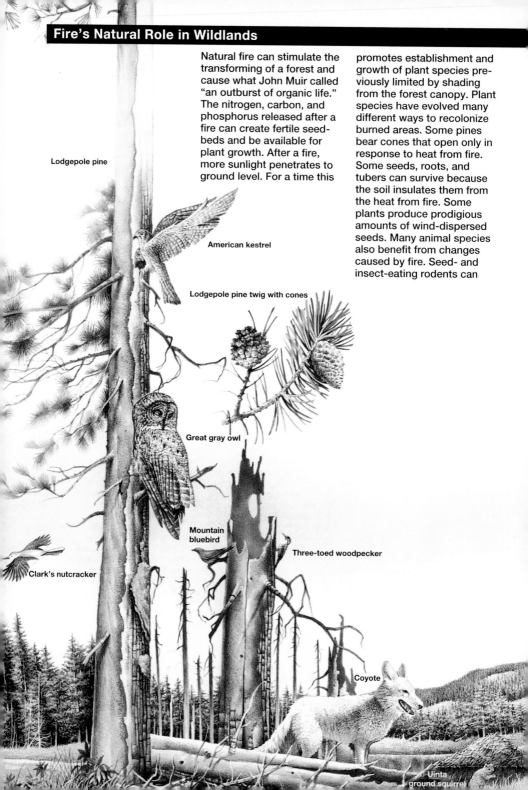

Fire's Natural Role in Wildlands

Natural fire can stimulate the transforming of a forest and cause what John Muir called "an outburst of organic life." The nitrogen, carbon, and phosphorus released after a fire can create fertile seedbeds and be available for plant growth. After a fire, more sunlight penetrates to ground level. For a time this promotes establishment and growth of plant species previously limited by shading from the forest canopy. Plant species have evolved many different ways to recolonize burned areas. Some pines bear cones that open only in response to heat from fire. Some seeds, roots, and tubers can survive because the soil insulates them from the heat from fire. Some plants produce prodigious amounts of wind-dispersed seeds. Many animal species also benefit from changes caused by fire. Seed- and insect-eating rodents can

Lodgepole pine

American kestrel

Lodgepole pine twig with cones

Great gray owl

Mountain bluebird

Three-toed woodpecker

Clark's nutcracker

Coyote

Uinta ground squirrel

increase in recent burns, and hawks or owls can hunt them more easily through the more open forest canopy. Mountain bluebirds take advantage of the new nest holes, and woodpeckers find more abundant sources of insect food in the remaining snag trees. Grazers like elk and bison and browsers like moose and deer take advantage of the better quality of forage, and this ultimately benefits predators and scavengers, too. The large illustration shows the landscape three years after a fire, when a heavy growth of fireweed,

aster, elk sedge, and some 20 other plants covers the forest floor. Lodgepole pine and aspen have established seedlings. Researchers have learned that fire returns to lodgepole pine forests at 200- to 400-year intervals but that fires of the scale experienced in 1988 may happen much less often.

The 1988 fires in and around Yellowstone gave scientists (right) a rare opportunity to study fire's effects on a very large scale.

Tree Ring Record of Fire Intervals

Recent fire damage

Normal ring growth

Early fire damage

Red-tailed hawk

Elk

cumbed to a temporary food shortage during the ensuing harsh winter. The fires also provided an unprecedented opportunity to study the effects of such large-scale burning on such a little-disturbed ecosystem.

The park's attempts to restore natural regulation have generated unquestioned successes as well as controversies. Today's free-roaming bison are much closer to the "vignette of primitive America" which the Leopold Report had recommended than were the fences, corrals, and hayfields used in the past. Perhaps the most striking success was with Yellowstone Lake's native cutthroat trout. The cutthroat's yearly spawning-runs up park streams are a spectacular and unusual phenomenon in their own right. They also are vital to white pelicans, ospreys, otters, and some 30 other wildlife species. The spawning runs had almost vanished in the early 1960s because of human fishing and hatchery removals. When fishing was regulated and hatcheries discontinued, however, these native trout returned in strength; by the 1980s the lake's cutthroats were providing a world-class sport fishery for people as well as a vital food source for grizzlies—as bears emerging from hibernation fed on fish packed into spawning streams.

This grizzly-trout interaction was a particularly hopeful development. It reunited two links of the primal Yellowstone ecosystem, links that artificial bear-feeding and fishery manipulation had all but parted. As Paul Schullery noted in *Mountain Time*, "Yellowstone is widely used as an example of what progressive management can do to turn around a deteriorating fishery."

Yet no success is final in wildlife management, because natural change and human pressures are continual. In 1994 park biologists were horrified to discover that fish-eating, non-native lake trout had been introduced illegally into Yellowstone Lake at least 20 years earlier.

The huge trout, which can grow to three feet long, had been quietly establishing spawning areas, and they seemed set to explode through the ecosystem with catastrophic effects on the smaller cutthroat on which they would prey. Fisheries experts predicted in 1995 that the native trout were likely to decline by 80 or 90 percent. Furthermore, such a precipitous drop in the cutthroat population threatened corresponding collapses in the lake watershed's entire web of life—for birds, otters, bears, *and* fly-fishing enthusiasts. Because lake trout live and spawn so deep in the lake, they will not replace cutthroats as prey for other park wildlife or for stream-fishing humans. The National Park Service will have to try to reduce the lake trout to some manageable level through measures like intensive gill-netting of their spawning areas. Whoever introduced the lake trout has caused economic and ecological problems that will persist into the foreseeable future.

The attempt to restore Yellowstone to its 2,000-year-old diversity continues despite such setbacks. In March 1995 wolves were reintroduced after 20 years of controversy as to whether livestock losses outside the park would outweigh the ecological and scientific values of having North America's greatest wilderness symbol inside the park. Although mountain lions had reinhabited Yellowstone naturally, the closest substantial population of the endangered Rocky Mountain wolf subspecies lived in northern Montana. Biologists thought it was unlikely that the wolves would return to Yellowstone unaided.

As part of a recovery plan to reintroduce them to the West, the U.S. Fish and Wildlife Service and the National Park Service transported 14 wolves captured in central Alberta to holding pens in several parts of the park. Released in April 1995, the animals surprised even experts with their ready adaptation. By May thousands of visitors were treated to the spectacle of big black or gray wolves chasing elk across the Lamar Valley in broad daylight. That sight had been virtually unknown in the West for 150 years.

"One of the criticisms of the program was that people would never see the wolves," Paul Schullery told me in 1996. "We had no idea it would be this good."

Seventeen more wolves arrived in 1996, this time from British Columbia. The goal was establishment of a self-sustaining park population of about 10 packs by 2002. Even when this is accomplished, Yellowstone wolves will never be as easy to see as elk or bison—but knowing that these highly social and intelligent creatures are there adds another dimension to the place.

On our way from Mammoth to the Lamar Valley

Native Fish and the Impacts of Exotic Species

When Yellowstone became a national park in 1872, only about 10 percent of its lakes contained fish. Arctic grayling, three types of cutthroat trout, mountain whitefish, three suckers, four minnows, and mottled sculpin were native to park waters. Between 1889 and 1955 native and non-native sport fish were widely stocked into numerous, previously fishless park waters to provide more recreational fishing. Hatcheries were set up for native fish and popular non-native sport fish—rainbow trout, brown trout, brook trout, Atlantic salmon, and black bass. Many of the stocking efforts failed, but the long-term effects remain. Interbreeding and competition with exotic species displaced native fish species and also disrupted stream and lake ecology. Some predators were deprived of their fish as food

sources. Yellowstone Lake is home to native Yellowstone cutthroat trout (below) that provide food for the grizzly bears, otters, mink, bald eagles, white pelicans, ospreys, and loons. Unfortunately, in 1994 illegally introduced lake trout were found in the lake. Lake trout prey on cutthroats and could reduce their numbers in this key, core habitat by at least 50 percent within 20 years if they are not suppressed. Bears, eagles, and other natural predators could suffer from the reduction of cutthroats because cutthroats spawn in streams and rivers —where predators can catch them. Lake trout do not spawn in streams and are not available to these predator species. Today Yellowstone continues to provide anglers the opportunity to try to catch wild fish in a natural setting, but long-term protection and restoration of native park fishes are now top priorities.

MCSimon
1979

one day, a park interpretive ranger described for me the three wolf packs through whose territory we were driving. The description was so detailed that it was almost as though we were passing through human communities. He also showed me where he had seen two gray wolves and a black one among the cottonwoods just a few days before. Now a bison herd was grazing there.

I talked to Paul Schullery about the original 1995 reintroduction. He mentioned seeing an elk placidly watching the truck caravan that brought the Alberta wolves into Yellowstone. "You have no idea what this means," Schullery had thought, silently addressing that unconcerned ungulate.

It does not mean that wolves by themselves will drastically reduce the elk populations. Even before wolves were returned, only about one of every three elk calves reached adulthood. In their first year elk calves are vulnerable to accidents, predators, and the effects of severe winter weather. But numbers remain high. Still, the return of the wolf almost certainly will result in a healthier elk population as wolves cull less fit individuals from the herd.

One of Yellowstone's smaller carnivores, the pine marten feeds primarily on small mammals, but its diet sometimes includes insects and berries.

Wildflowers

Lewis Monkeyflower

Prickly Pear Cactus

Indian Paintbrush

Marsh Marigold

Lupine

Fireweed

Phlox

Sticky Geranium

Shooting Star

Calypso Orchid

Arrowleaf Balsamroot

Bitterroot

Alpine Forget-Me-Not

Stonecrop

Birds and Mammals

Elk

Yellowheaded Blackbird

Pronghorn with young

Barrow's Goldeneye

Blue Grouse

Yellow Warbler

Mountain Lion

Pika

Trumpeter Swan

Badgers

Moose calf

Mountain Bluebird

Great Gray Owl

Bald Eagle

Greater Yellowstone

The most compelling wildlife experiences I've had at Yellowstone occurred outside the park boundary, in the remote mountains that ring the plateau. If the park's thermal fields are like the Earth's beginnings, those remote places are like all the millions of pre-civilized years that came after. I remember camping in a little meadow north of the Buffalo Plateau that felt as though no human had ever been there—only the moose that slipped through the surrounding forest so quietly they seemed to materialize from the deadfalls and pine boughs. A herd of elk filed up a distant slope like ancient silhouettes painted on a cave wall near Lascaux in France by humans before historic time. I didn't see as many elk there as I have while driving around the park, but there was an incomparable—and sometimes startling—intimacy about those remote places.

Some of the most intimate encounters occurred in sight of camp, as when a marten appeared hunting pikas in a scree pile, or flying squirrels sailed down to steal some food, or otters, two adults and a pair of pups, spent an afternoon playing in a small lake. Sometimes I felt as though I'd fallen down the rabbit hole in Lewis Carroll's story.

Along the Stillwater River, I encountered beaver dam-and-canal systems so extensive and solidly constructed that I first assumed the conservation corps or some other human agency had built them. Some of the dams looked 10 feet high. Camping on Hellroaring Creek, I heard sounds uncannily like people shouting and talking in the creek's roar, and my wife thought some huge animal was moving around our tent all night long. When she bent to tie her shoes next morning, she fell over backward. The "huge animal" had been a mouse that passed the night chewing her shoelaces into tidy, one-inch lengths.

While relatively few people visit them, such backcountry places are as vital to the park as Old Faithful or Yellowstone Lake. Established to include the geothermal features, an area of roughly 2.2 million acres, the park is large by any standard, but it's only a small rectangle in a roughly oval region that covers all or much of twelve counties in northwest Wyoming, southwest Montana, and eastern Idaho. Many of the things that distinguish Yellowstone National Park, including both hot springs and big wild animals, depend on resources beyond the park's boundary. Drilling for water or geothermal power outside the park, for example, could cause geysers inside the park to subside. In fact, this has happened to geyser fields elsewhere.

Conservationists recognized how important the "Greater Yellowstone" was as early as the 1880s, as resource exploitation increased outside the park. In 1891 the government began setting aside adjacent land, eventually the six national forests that now surround the park. Although open to some commercial activities, the national forests provided a degree of protection. They acted as a buffer to more intensively used private lands. Ruggedness and inaccessibility largely kept them wild, without roads or other developments, and park animals could move onto them and still be fairly safe from hunting. As population grew during the 20th century, however, pressures on wildlands intensified.

By 1930 roads and farms had cut off the park's grizzly bears from populations farther north. In effect, the Yellowstone region was becoming an island of wildland surrounded by more tamed areas. As biologists have learned, such islands can prove to be unreliable refuges for wildlife. If disease or other mortality factors lower a species' numbers within such an "island" setting, that species is liable to die out there because more individuals can't move in and supplement the local population.

Isolated populations tend to become inbred. Inherited genetic defects also can endanger their survival. The smaller such an island is, the fewer the species it will support in the long run.

Fortunately the Yellowstone region is a very big island, although it is unclear exactly how big. A cooperative National Park Service and Forest Service group, the Greater Yellowstone Coordinating Committee, defined it at just under 12 million acres in 1987, but a citizen's advocacy group, the Greater Yellowstone Coalition, defined it as nearly double that in 1996. By any reckoning the Yellowstone region often is called the most intact wildland ecosystem in the world's north temperate zone, and there probably is no other place in the North American or Eurasian mid-latitudes where such diversity of native wildlife is protected. Yet isolation makes even it vulnerable.

There has been great concern that grizzlies might just gradually disappear like they have in smaller parks. Is the number of grizzlies remaining in the entire Yellowstone region large enough for indefinite survival? Nobody knows—grizzlies were considered part of the fauna of Yosemite, Sequoia, and Mount Rainier when those national parks were established in the 1890s. Nevertheless, the trapping and hunting in nearby areas had eliminated those grizzlies by the 1920s. "There aren't many people who believe that a grizzly bear can survive if it has only the park itself as habitat," Paul Schullery has written.

The grizzly situation has driven conservationists to think increasingly in regional terms. Bear researcher John Craighead began using the term "Greater Yellowstone Ecosystem" in the 1960s. Now it has gained general currency. Enhancing the protection of natural resources within the entire ecosystem has become a goal for organizations such as the Greater Yellowstone Coordinating Committee and Greater Yellowstone Coalition. Grizzlies aren't the only species here with an isolated population. The park's pronghorns are thought to be cut off from others on down the Yellowstone Valley, and in past decades their numbers have dropped dangerously low at times. The region also provides the only significant wintering habitat in the lower 48 states for the trumpeter swan, the world's largest swan. At least the grizzlies, pronghorns, and swans have sizeable natural populations elsewhere, unlike the Yellowstone cutthroat trout. The cutthroat now is reduced to 15 percent of its original range in the Yellowstone and Snake river drainages.

Increasing the amount of protected land in the region has been one way to conserve resources. In 1882 General Philip Sheridan proposed more than doubling the park's size to "make a preserve for the large game of the West, now rapidly decreasing." Sheridan's suggestion was ignored, but park bound-

Greater Yellowstone Ecosystem

Congress drew the national park boundary in 1872 to protect geysers, hot springs, and other scenic features from development. The park was enlarged in the 1920s to protect winter range of elk and other hoofed mammals (ungulates). Park managers today hope to provide visitors with a look not just at scenic features but also at networks of dynamic ecological processes, valuable in and of themselves. How the park's component parts are related to one another may play out over vast areas. They can't be constrained by jurisdictional boundaries, or they cease to be natural and wild. It is neither possible nor desirable to protect populations of wide-ranging carnivores—cougars, wolverines, and grizzlies—solely within Yellowstone National Park. For example, part of the year many of Yellowstone's bears feed on army cutworm moths near the highest summits. Yet the moths winter on the plains. To preserve grizzlies requires protecting them and their food on a large scale and on a regional basis. The Greater Yellowstone Ecosystem encompasses the entire elevated plateau at whose heart the park rests (see the inset map). This ecosystem is the home to recovering populations of gray wolves and grizzly bears and to one of North America's largest

A B S A R O K A

Yellowstone Lake

Hayden Valley

Shoshone Lake

This panorama, looking due east, was created by draping a satellite image on a digital model of the landscape.

elk herds as well as five other ungulate species, coyotes, red foxes, bobcats, and dozens of smaller mammals. But elk migrate, bears roam, and non-native plants' seeds ride on the wind. Ecosystem management challenges us to devise policies that work across multiple boundaries and interests. And here this means six national forests, two national parks, three national wildlife refuge areas, an Indian reservation, Bureau of Land Management lands, and state and private lands in three states. Throughout this broad geographic area hydrologists work along lines of river drainages and mountain ranges, while ethnographers search out patterns among human tribes and cultures. Wildland fire managers, foresters, and bird biologists work across jurisdictions to monitor and manage the shared resources. The whole of this Greater Yellowstone Ecosystem is indeed far greater than the sum of its parts.

National Park Service

U.S. Forest Service

U.S. Fish and Wildlife Service

TETON National Wilderness Preservation System

Lands administered by the **U.S. Bureau of Land Management** and by **states** are not shown.

aries were extended to include some headwaters and winter range in the 1920s. In 1912 the federal government established the National Elk Refuge in Jackson Hole to provide winter range for the park's southern herds. Those elk had been in conflict with livestock. In 1929 Congress established the adjacent Grand Teton National Park where that steep range rises above the Snake River. Two other national wildlife refuges, Red Rock Lakes and Grays Lake, also protect habitat for trumpeter swans and cranes, and the U.S. Bureau of Land Management, Wind River Indian Reservation, and state parks and refuges also conserve thousands of acres.

As important as parks and refuges is designated wilderness, a category of management that excludes roads, machinery, and other uses from some federal public lands. The Forest Service began designating wilderness areas administratively in the 1920s, and Congress created a National Wilderness Preservation System through passage of the Wilderness Act in 1964. Nearly four million acres of designated wilderness exist in the national forests around the parks, so that both Yellowstone and Grand Teton national parks are now half surrounded by wilderness. The places where I encountered those romping otters and engineering beavers are in the Absaroka-Beartooth Wilderness of the Gallatin and Custer national forests. Most of the two national parks also is recommended and managed as wilderness, even though Congress had not yet designated wilderness within these parklands by the year 2000.

Almost half of the conservatively-estimated, 12-million-acre version of the Greater Yellowstone Ecosystem is either designated wilderness or recommended for protection as wilderness. But this means more than half is not. Forty-four percent of the ecosystem, including much of the designated wilderness, is open to livestock grazing all or part of the year. Most of the national forest lands that are not designated or recommended as wilderness have been or will be logged. Almost all of Targhee National Forest on Yellowstone Park's west side is logged, making a sharp contrast along the park border. Forty percent of the Greater Yellowstone Ecosystem is open to mineral leasing. Seventeen percent is under lease for gas, oil, or phosphate mining. What is more, the road building associated with this grazing, logging, and mining activity only amplifies and intensifies the pressure on wildlife by providing vehicular access to remote areas. Hunting is legal on public lands outside parks and refuges (and even in part of Grand Teton National Park). This can affect sensitive species such as the grizzly; a few grizzlies are accidentally or intentionally shot nearly every year. And where winter once gave wildlife seasonal respite from mechanized disturbance, snowmobiles and snowcoaches changed that. Air quality is also a growing concern. Researchers measure air pollution by analyzing mountain snowpack for airborne pollutants like sulfates, nitrates, and acid. High concentrations have been found near Yellowstone.

Several million acres of privately owned land in the Greater Yellowstone Ecosystem generate some of the greatest pressures on its resources. A trend toward more intensive use has led to subdivision of many former ranches—for second-home communities, golf courses, and ski resorts. In the mid-1990s a Canadian company planned to develop a vast gold, silver, and copper mine less than three miles from the park's northeast boundary at the headwaters of three pristine streams. Public interest in these concerns was intense, and a buyout of the mining property was approved by Congress in 1998. Also in the mid-1990s Montana approved development of a geothermal well on a large private property less than two miles from the park's northwest boundary.

The proliferation of such pressures raises serious questions about the ability of the Greater Yellowstone Ecosystem to survive as that "most intact temperate ecosystem" referred to earlier.

"Many of us here are convinced that at least the short-term prognosis for the Yellowstone grizzly is pretty bright," said John Varley, director of the Yellowstone Center for Resources, in an interview with bear authority Steve Herrero in 1995. "But we don't know anybody, at least not anybody with a reasonably sound perspective on the future, who thinks that the long-term prospects for the grizzly bear in greater Yellowstone are anything but grim. The grizzly bear is resilient enough to handle ski areas, or hard rock mining, but nobody with even half a brain believes that the bear is resilient enough to handle the entire array of civilization encroachment that we're seeing here."

Restoring Wolves

When the national park was established in 1872 gray wolves were native to Yellowstone. Throughout much of the West larger wildlife species—bison, elk, and deer—were fast disappearing and being replaced by livestock. Wolves, coyotes, bears, and mountain lions had no choice but to prey on livestock. By the late 1800s predator control was the norm throughout the West, even in this park. At least 136 wolves were killed in Yellowstone between 1914 and 1926. By the 1940s sightings of wolf packs were rare. An intensive survey showed no evidence of a viable wolf population here in 1975. And so, for many years, of the known species that lived in the park in the 1700s, only the gray wolf was missing from Yellowstone. Following the 1973 Endangered Species Act, National Park Service policy directs that native species should be restored to a park if certain conditions are met: there must be enough habitat to promise success, and serious threats to outside interests must be preventable. Detailed studies and plans for restoring the wolf to Yellowstone and parts of Idaho began in the 1980s. In 1995, 14 Canadian wolves from three separate family groups or packs were transplanted to Yellowstone, and 17 more were transplanted the next year. By 1997 the number of packs had grown from three to nine in the Greater Yellowstone Ecosystem. Three years later more than 115 wolves inhabited the Greater Yellowstone Ecosystem, and nearly 330 wolves lived throughout the Rocky Mountain tri-state recovery area.

As Varley implied, the task of keeping the Yellowstone ecosystem healthy will not get easier. When Congress was debating the original park bill in 1872, one of its supporters' arguments was that the park was "worthless land," too remote, high, and cold to be farmed, so leaving it alone would not have economic costs. While crops are impractical in a land with regular summer frosts, Yellowstone's water, timber, thermal fields, and other features are far from worthless. Farm interests tried to dam and divert park waters for irrigation throughout the first half of the 20th century, and there have been many other attempts to commercialize park resources. Yellowstone has always had its costs, and will continue to have them, both the costs of protecting wild resources and of foregoing commercial exploitation. If lake trout destroy the Yellowstone Lake fishery, for example, what would be the cost to restore it? This would require removing the introduced species and building up a cutthroat population again. Estimates were between $32 million and $181 million, based on 1990s figures. And even if lake trout can be controlled, protecting the fishery over the next 30 years will cost an estimated $30 million.

Smaller programs such as wolf reintroduction also have price tags. Yellowstone wolves have killed some livestock, and have themselves been killed by poachers and vehicles. Ironically the wolves' deaths have been much more costly than have livestock losses, considering the expense of importing the wolves. Yet in a world where large wild animals are dwindling everywhere, an important predator's return to this "most intact temperate ecosystem" has a significance transcending its projected cost. If the world's richest nation can't have one of its great carnivores in its most famous national park, how can we expect poorer nations to keep their lions, jaguars, and tigers? On the other hand, if the United States values the wholeness of its wildlands enough to devote money and effort to restoring the wolf, then it brings hope to national parks everywhere.

Should the grizzly eventually disappear from Yellowstone, it will be more than a regional loss, or even a national loss. In 1976 Yellowstone National Park was designated a biosphere reserve, the United States' first. Biosphere reserves are areas of global ecological concern in which interactions between humans and wildlands are seen as particularly vital. In 1978 the park was designated a world heritage site, placing it on a level with the Galapagos Islands and Australia's Great Barrier Reef as a "wonder of the world"—a place "of outstanding universal value from the viewpoint of science, conservation, or natural beauty." The park is one of only about a hundred world heritage sites on Earth, so protecting it certainly seems worthwhile. Conservationists have suggested that the park might be better protected if the biosphere reserve included the entire 12 million (or 20 million) acres of the Greater Yellowstone Ecosystem. Indeed, the urgency of protecting the larger area seemed ever more important when Yellowstone was placed on the list of endangered world heritage sites.

World's Greatest Geyser Collection

If Yellowstone's thermal features all suddenly fell silent, the world's total number of geysers would plummet. Seven major basins here—one of only two essentially undisturbed geyser areas on Earth—hold approximately two-thirds of the world's geysers. Altogether there are more than 300 geysers here and more than 10,000 thermal features: geysers, hot springs, mudpots, and fumaroles (see also pages 36 to 39).

The world's tallest active geyser, Steamboat, is in the Norris Geyser Basin. Its rare, pulsating, memorable eruptions burst as much as 250 to nearly 400 feet in the air. The Upper Geyser Basin features Old Faithful, Grand, Castle, Giantess, Beehive, and Lion geysers.

Naturalist John Muir dubbed the vast, volcanic Yellowstone Plateau "this good fire mountain." The park and its geyser basins have been called Geyserland, Fairyland, and Wonderland. However, companies in the past have applied for geothermal leases on lands outside the park boundary that are known to have geothermal resources. To what extent are these resources connected to the national park's thermal features? Would drilling west and north of the park disrupt or diminish the thermal features inside Yellowstone?

Research is urgently needed on these questions. Rapid or dramatic change in energy economics could create pressure to open nearby areas to drilling, with potentially disastrous consequences for park thermal features.

Cupric Caldron

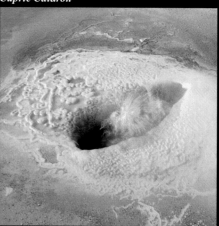

A perpetually splashing hot spring

Canary Spring

Clepsydra Geyser

A red hot spring near Mud Volcano

Punch Bowl Spring flow

Grotto Geyser

Violet Hot Springs mudpot

Along the Firehole River

Steamboat Geyser

Grand Geyser

Castle Geyser

Lion Geyser and Heart Spring

Riverside Geyser

Cliff Geyser

Old Faithful Geyser

Unforeseen Values
Of Preservation

Yellowstone became the world's first national park when Congress passed and the President signed the 1872 law. Most nations have now established park systems, and this national park idea has been called the best idea America ever had. Yet the members of Congress who voted on the Yellowstone bill would have been surprised to learn they had done something so important. The bill is two paragraphs long. It simply describes a "tract of land . . . near the headwaters of the Yellowstone River" and declares it "reserved and withdrawn from settlement, occupancy, or sale under the Laws of the United States, and dedicated and set apart as a public park or pleasuring ground for the benefit and enjoyment of the people." Another paragraph of amendments concerns preserving "timber, mineral deposits, natural curiosities or wonders" and preventing "wanton destruction of fish and game," but the amendments are pretty vague. This is a very sketchy blueprint for an institution—national parks—that now covers more than four percent of United States territory and even larger percentages of some other nations.

It probably is fair to say that the United States did not know what a national park was when it created the world's first. The meaning of the term has more or less grown up since and is still unclear. To many, for example, a national park is simply a place with scenery and wildlife where people go to have fun. Yet such places have existed throughout history, although usually they've been reserved for privileged elites rather than available to everybody, as national parks are. The national park's democratic dimension is an important part of its meaning, but that is not definitive either. National forests are places with scenery and wildlife, open to everyone, but they are different because they produce timber and other commodities.

What do national parks produce? "The benefit and enjoyment of the people," as Congress said, but

105

what exactly are these concepts? In the past 125 years, Congress's two paragraphs have been putting out new meanings. As a result, Yellowstone has been a "messenger from Earth" in more than a geological sense. Other messages have spun off from its central geological message. The park has been a book of life as well as of rocks. It is one of the last relatively unabridged books of life in the north temperate zone.

From the geological and biological messages a historical message emerged. Yellowstone's dramatic and pristine landscape, like the "lost world" in an adventure story, has presented industrial civilization with a vision of what it will lose if it lets the old, wild Earth slip away. The park not only marks a possible turning point in worldwide human history but has a history of its own. Its visitors and its custodians have interpreted and reinterpreted its meaning and used those interpretations in experiencing and managing the park.

If the 1872 Yellowstone law was the seed from which the national park has grown, Yellowstone was its first seedling. Many of the things parks would accomplish and the problems they would face happened here first. Every park in the world has its special accomplishments and problems, yet Yellowstone perhaps has enough of the aura of all parks about it to serve as a paradigm.

The main "benefit and enjoyment" Yellowstone always provided the people has been the right to go there—tourism. Nature tourism existed before Yellowstone, although never on such a scale. That scale has helped revolutionize humanity's attitude toward wild nature. It also has created so many difficulties that tourism has been the park's greatest challenge as well as its main benefit.

The challenge already had begun with passage of the park bill. Congress did not mandate or fund management, and poachers, squatters, and vandals were breaking the new law even as President Grant signed it. The first superintendent, park advocate Nathaniel Langford, proved ineffectual because he had to make his living elsewhere. His successor in 1877, wealthy and eccentric frontiersman Philetus Norris, managed to wrest road-building appropriations from Congress but little else. The result of this neglect was that early tourists and the concessioners who served them did anything they wanted. They hunted meat, plowed meadows for crops, cut trees for construction, and threw everything from soap to wagon wheels into the hot springs and geysers for fun. No officials existed to stop them until Congress finally appropriated funds in 1882, and then most were unqualified political appointees. The visitors' antics overwhelmed the competent few like Kansan Josiah Weimer, who found their desire to abuse geysers, litter, and leave campfires "unabating and determined."

Things were so bad by 1886 that the government called in the Cavalry. This may seem like a drastic solution to vandalism, but with no major wars to distract it, the Army did a good job of running the park for three decades. It established Fort Yellowstone at Mammoth Hot Springs, whose foursquare frame and stone buildings stand a little incongruously under Mount Everts as though on loan from the U.S. Military Academy at West Point.

The fort administered a parkwide system of outposts staffed not only during the tourist season but in winter, when poachers went after elk teeth (prized by fraternal lodges) and bison heads (used as barroom decorations). To discourage troopers from poaching on their own as they patrolled on skis, they were required to account for every bullet fired. Soldiers also registered visitors at park entrances and policed thermal basins, sometimes forcing vandals to scrub out initials carved into the geyser rims. Winter patrols saved Yellowstone's bison, and the park itself perhaps owes its continuance to the Cavalry—no other force existed to protect it from the growing pressures. By World War I, however, the relative stability prevailing since 1886 shifted again. The Army faced other commitments, and tourism was poised to explode beyond the record of 10,000 annual visitors reached in 1897.

Early Yellowstone tourists fell into two groups: the "carriage trade," well-to-do visitors who arrived in packaged, railroad tours; and the "sagebrushers," who roughed it in their own tents and wagons. The former was expensive and the latter strenuous, so tourism stayed at levels the military could handle. The private automobile promised to change all that.

Grudgingly, the Army admitted the automobile to the park in 1915, but the new National Park Service,

Next pages: *Photographers from around the world are attracted to Yellowstone's wildlife. Maintaining a safe distance from animals is the key to capturing their natural, undisturbed behavior.*

which took over for good in 1918, welcomed it. Created two years earlier under the leadership of millionaire public relations expert Stephen Tyng Mather, the National Park Service promoted tourism where the Army had resisted it. It reasoned that exposure to America's natural wonders offered an antidote to urban stresses for the nation's increasingly industrialized population. The Model T of National Park Service supporter Henry Ford proved the practical vehicle for further democratizing the Yellowstone experience. The motorist supplanted the sagebrusher. Railroad-based carriage trade lingered through the 1930s, but buses, not carriages, made the park tours. The annual visitation rose steadily from 51,895 in 1915 to 260,697 in 1929.

The National Park Service continued the Army's vigorous opposition to poaching, vandalism, and other lawbreaking. However, it tended to be permissive toward popular activities like fishing and wildlife-feeding.

"At the park camps and around the kitchens of the hotels," wrote 1919 visitor Alma White, "black, brown, and occasionally grizzly bears could be seen at almost any hour of the day eating out of tins. . . ." The National Park Service built bleachers beside dumps so the visitors could watch bears eat garbage. Horace Albright was park superintendent from 1919 to 1929. He personified this era of the "good host." A Mather protégé whose zeal for publicity outdid even his mentor's, Albright liked to drop in and chat with the tourists at their campsites. He once allowed Hollywood to use the park's bison to stage a stampede for a movie called *The Thundering Herd.* That drew thunder from conservationists.

The "good host" tourism model lasted through the 1930s and early 1940s, partly because the Depression and World War II kept visitation at manageable levels, with a peak of a half million in 1940. Annual visits soared in the affluent post-war period, however, climbing above one million in 1948 and averaging over two million after 1960. Yellowstone no longer could sustain the easy-going 1920s style, and the quality of fishing, thermal fields, and concessions declined from sheer force of numbers. With no apparent option to restrict the visitation, and in response to growing public litigiousness, the park's managers had to adopt a more cautious stance. This sometimes led to controversy, too, as when dump-closures led to increased bear-people confrontations in the early 1970s, and then to a less visible bear population as the animals recovered their reliance on wild foods. Even international visitors still sometimes complain "Where are the bears?"

Today's millions of Yellowstone visitors will necessarily have a somewhat different experience than did the thousands of a century ago. An 1890s tourist could, and sometimes did, spend an entire summer camping in the park, but space limitations and dramatically increased visitation make this difficult today. Even the average 19th-century visitor spent weeks in the park—today's visitor spends, on average, a day and a half. Early visitors roamed virtually at will among the geyser fields and sometimes cooked food or washed clothes in hot springs, while today's visitor stays on boardwalks and scenic drives in the main geyser fields.

Still, there probably has been more continuity than change in the Yellowstone experience. Historian Richard Bartlett found early tourists "mere counterparts of today's visitors" in many ways. "They were busy snapping pictures; they waxed enthusiastic over hot springs and geysers." Modern tourists follow the same "grand loop" route through the park first mapped out by the 1869-1871 expeditions. Both route and attractions are little changed. However, in the years ahead we must figure out how to meet the challenge of accommodating the ever-growing popularity of a national park experience without impairing the park or the experience.

Some changes have enhanced continuity—reviving features heavy traffic had frayed. Restored from their 1950s slump, the Lake Hotel and Old Faithful Inn are valued historic structures and provide visitor services comparable to those of the 1920s. Thanks to the boardwalks, geyser fields now display vegetation and formations more like what the earliest visitors saw—not the scuffed and trampled areas seen some 50 or more years ago.

I was surprised at how much the boardwalks contributed to my appreciation of thermal areas. I usually feel that a natural feature is best left to itself at the end of a long trail, but at Yellowstone I was more impressed with the easily reached geothermal fields than backcountry ones like Monument Geyser

Page 114: *Anglers seek out Yellowstone in autumn when cool conditions bring out late hatches of aquatic insects.*

Page 115: *When boiling water meets subzero air, the results are spectacular. If the wind is right, Grand Geyser's winter eruptions may shower bystanders with ice crystals.*

Thermophiles: Geothermal Microbes

Hot springs are full of unique life forms that have inhabited Earth nearly 4 billion years. A pool's many colors mostly derive from light refraction, suspended mineral particles, and large communities of primitive life forms: microscopic algae, bacteria, and *Archaea*. (The *Archaea*, once considered bacteria, have completely different DNA.) They grow in water too hot for most kinds of life familiar to us on Earth. Life even occurs in boiling water, but, as the water cools to about 160°F (72°C), the organisms

become rich, thick, living layers of color in many different hues. The chemistry of thermal pools also influences the kinds and abundance of life. The boiling hot springs of Norris, which are more acidic than battery acid, sustain algae, bacteria, and *Archaea* far different from those living in the alkaline springs in the Old Faithful area. Collectively called thermophiles, these bizarre life forms are still largely a mystery to scientists. How do they thrive in such hostile environments? What can

they teach us about present and past life on Earth or elsewhere in the universe? Because of the great scientific interest in thermophiles, studies occasionally lead to the discovery of processes or products that have value in our society. One famous example is the laboratory cloning of a heat-stable enzyme originally produced from a minute sample of the Yellowstone microbe named *Thermus aquaticus*. This novel enzyme, now known as Taq Polymerase, is mass-produced in laboratories for

use in DNA studies throughout the world. A seemingly
small discovery in a Yellowstone hot spring ultimately
made a major contribution to
the scientific revolution in
DNA analysis in law enforcement, medicine, and agricul-
ture. Below and at right, biologists cautiously sample
thermal pools for thermo-
philic organisms. To do this
research, biologists must
obtain special permits, and
their work is closely super-
vised by Yellowstone's staff.

Basin on the ridge above Gibbon Meadows. Monument Geyser Basin has been called "one of the strangest spots in the park." Tombstone-like, the sinter structures for which it is named are indeed impressive. (Sinter forms when mineral-rich waters cool and evaporate.) Yet I didn't feel that this area's undeveloped seclusion was much of an advantage. It was still somewhat trampled, and I felt insecure about how best to see it—and somehow tempted to mill around and trample more. At Mud Volcano or Mammoth, on the other hand, I didn't itch to wander in search of the best vantage points, because the boardwalks showed them.

Far from obscuring natural settings, the boardwalks enhance them. They provide a kind of frame, a self-guiding context. Indeed, one underemphasized aspect of the Yellowstone experience is that park management is as much art as science. The science side gets a lot of attention because it deals with the resources themselves, while the art side deals with the visitor's enjoyment of them. Unlike most 20th-century art, park management struggles to draw attention not to itself but only to its subject. And so it might seem insignificant. "Where's the art in a boardwalk?" you might ask. I found out on the Norris Geyser Basin boardwalk when an elk herd took over a section for an hour.

As I stood with the ranger on duty waiting to get back to the parking lot, she mentioned in passing that the boardwalk-builder was a sculptor who put as much of himself into their siting and structuring as into his studio pieces. She didn't tell me his name, but then the sculptors who decorated medieval cathedrals were anonymous, and these two arts seem similar in purpose.

Certainly tourism will remain the most important way the public enjoys the park, but there is much more to "the benefit of the people" than recreation. And this "more" can come from unexpected quarters in always-strange Yellowstone. The most spectacular example may be *Thermus aquaticus*, the humble hot-spring bacterium mentioned earlier.

Microbiologist Thomas D. Brock discovered the species in Mushroom Pool at the Lower Geyser Basin in the 1960s. Brock deposited specimens in the American Type Culture Collection, making it available to researchers. Two decades later, a biotechnology company extracted an enzyme called Taq Polymerase from Brock's material. Because *T. aquaticus* is adapted to hot water, the enzyme functions at the high temperatures of a process called the Polymerase Chain Reaction (PCR), in which strands of genetic material, DNA, are replicated at high speed. PCR has become the basis of a multimillion-dollar biotechnology industry, commonly known as DNA fingerprinting, which allows biologists to identify organisms far more quickly and accurately than ever before. It has been applied to diagnosing many diseases, including AIDS. It also has wide legal and biological applications: individuals and species can be identified from a few cells.

T. aquaticus and now several other hot spring microorganisms promise valuable industrial applications. Some may help clean up oil spills or search for life on other planets. Hundreds probably will prove helpful one day. Not even 10 percent of Yellowstone's thermal microbe residents were identified by 1996, despite the more than 40 studies looking for new ones. One benefit of national parks that has achieved prominence recently is that of preserving biodiversity—the whole array of a country's ecosystems. We usually associate this with exotic ecosystems such as tropical rainforests, but Yellowstone's microorganisms are among the best examples so far. Had the park's diverse thermal habitats not been preserved from destruction, these crucial discoveries might not have been made.

"Even other volcanic areas such as Iceland, Japan and New Zealand, do not have the riches that we find in Yellowstone," Brock writes. "The main reason . . . is that Yellowstone's thermal features have been protected from destruction. In the other major thermal areas of the world, which also include Italy, geothermal power developments and health spas have taken over and destroyed the natural thermal features. This is why scientists from other countries come to Yellowstone. They know that the thermal features here are intact for all to see and explore."

Members of Congress who voted for the 1872 national park bill would be pleased to know how their decision to put science, scenery, and patriotism above commerce and property at Yellowstone paid off with tiny *Thermus aquaticus*. I doubt they'd be surprised it paid off. In keeping with their optimistic

century, they expected scientific wonders to flow from natural wonders like those at Yellowstone.

Such payoffs are by no means the end of the challenges Yellowstone poses for civilization. While everyone benefits from PCR technology, for example, how should its financial rewards be distributed? Conservationists increasingly feel that industries profiting from resources such as Yellowstone's microbes should contribute to protecting them. The National Park Service is now exploring how companies seeking valuable organisms in parks might allocate some of the rewards to managing those parks. But this is a complex matter. Researchers don't cart hot springs off to their labs—they collect samples of water or organic material. In effect, they mine information, not commodities. The question then becomes: how do we put a price on that?

Still, collecting this data that sparks multimillion-dollar industries certainly is a form of commercial development, however impossible to anticipate from traditional ideas of national parks as an escape from industrialism's stresses.

Yellowstone will go on producing things not envisioned in traditional ideas of national parks. If the park is a messenger from the Earth's past, perhaps, in this respect, it is also a messenger from its future.

I find it significant that in the ancient world oracles often were located in places like Yellowstone, in wild mountains where the Earth smokes. Yellowstone is a kind of oracle. It's a conduit of wisdom from deep, mysterious places to living people. Yellowstone is an oracle to world civilization and an oracle to every visitor who looks into a geyser pool and wonders at the heavenly blue light seeming to come from below. It reminds us, as oracles were meant to do, that human beings are part of the universal interplay of change and continuance that the ancients called "fate." It reminds us that Yellowstone's story is also our story. We, too, are messengers from Earth.

Each of Yellowstone's 10,000 thermal features is a unique combination of form, color, and activity. But none is frozen in time; change, driven by earthquakes and other primal forces, is constant.

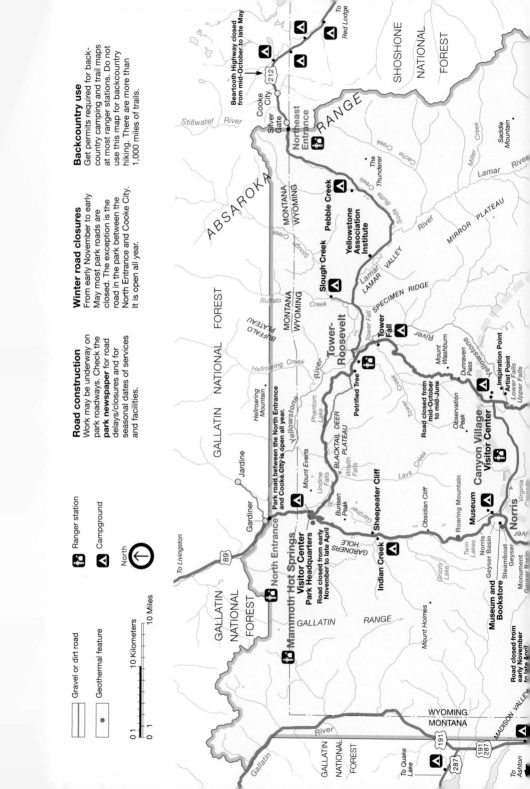

Backcountry use

Get permits required for back-country camping and trail maps at most ranger stations. Do not use this map for backcountry hiking. There are more than 1,000 miles of trails.

Winter road closures

From early November to early May most park roads are closed. The exception is the road in the park between the North Entrance and Cooke City. It is open all year.

Road construction

Work may be underway on park roadways. Check the **park newspaper** for road delays/closures and for seasonal dates of services and facilities.

Ranger station

Campground

Gravel or dirt road

Geothermal feature

North

10 Kilometers

10 Miles

SHOSHONE NATIONAL FOREST

To Red Lodge

Beartooth Highway closed from mid-October to late May

212

Cooke City

Silver Gate

Northeast Entrance

Stillwater River

ABSAROKA RANGE

Saddle Mountain

Miller Creek

Cache Creek

The Thunderer

Soda Butte Creek

Lamar River

Pebble Creek

Yellowstone Association Institute

MIRROR PLATEAU

Slough Creek

Slough Creek

Lamar River

LAMAR VALLEY

SPECIMEN RIDGE

MONTANA WYOMING

GALLATIN NATIONAL FOREST

Buffalo Creek

BUFFALO PLATEAU

Hellroaring Creek

Hellroaring Mountain

Yellowstone River

Phantom Lake

Tower-Roosevelt

Petrified Tree

Tower Fall

Tower Fall

Tower Creek

Mount Washburn

Dunraven Pass

Yellowstone River

Inspiration Point

Artist Point

Lower Falls

Upper Falls

Road closed from mid-October to mid-June

Observation Peak

Canyon Village Visitor Center

Park road between the North Entrance and Cooke City is open all year.

Jardine

Gardiner

To Livingston

89

North Entrance

Mammoth Hot Springs Visitor Center Park Headquarters

Road closed from early November to late April

GARDNERS HOLE

Mount Everts

Undine Falls

Bunsen Peak

Gardner River

Sheepeater Cliff

Indian Creek

BLACKTAIL DEER PLATEAU

Wraith Falls

Lava Creek

Obsidian Cliff

Roaring Mountain

Museum

Twin Lakes

Grizzly Lake

Norris Geyser Basin

Norris

Museum and Bookstore

Steamboat Geyser

Monument Geyser Basin

Virginia Cascade

Road closed from early November to late April

Mount Holmes

GALLATIN RANGE

GALLATIN NATIONAL FOREST

WYOMING MONTANA

191

To Quake Lake

Gallatin River

287

191 287

MADISON VALLEY

To Ashton

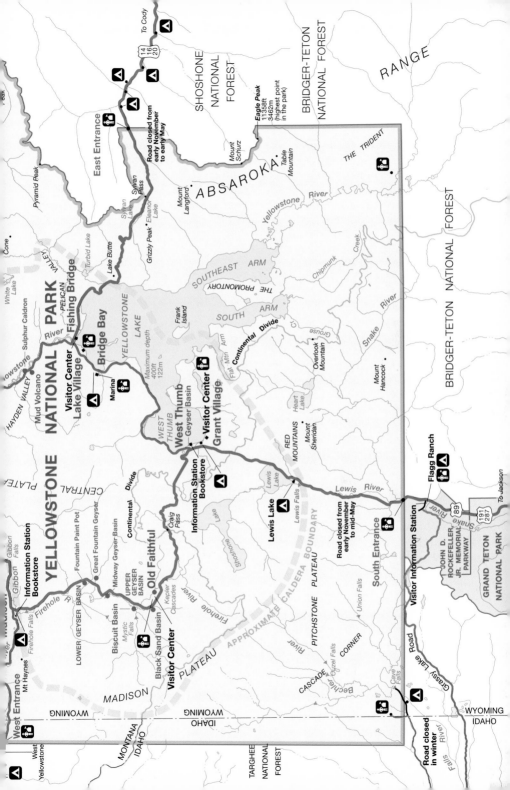

To Cody

14
16
20

SHOSHONE
NATIONAL
FOREST

BRIDGER-TETON
NATIONAL FOREST

RANGE

East Entrance

Road closed from
early November
to early May

Eagle Peak
11358ft
3462m
(highest point
in the park)

BRIDGER-TETON

THE TRIDENT

Mount
Schurz

ABSAROKA

Sylvan
Pass

Turbid Lake

Sylvan
Lake

Eleanor
Lake

Lake Butte

Grizzly Peak

Mount
Langford

*Table
Mountain*

Mount
Schurz

Pyramid Peak

NATIONAL

PELICAN VALLEY

Yellowstone

River

Chipmunk

Creek

Cone

White
Lake

SOUTHEAST ARM

THE PROMONTORY

FOREST

PARK

Fishing Bridge

Sulphur Caldron

HAYDEN VALLEY

River

YELLOWSTONE

Frank Island

SOUTH
ARM

Flat Mtn Arm

Continental Divide

Grouse

Overlook
Mountain

Snake

River

Mount
Hancock

YELLOWSTONE

Visitor Center
Lake Village

Bridge Bay

LAKE

Maximum depth
400ft
122m

Heart
Lake

Mud Volcano

Marina

Visitor Center
Grant Village

West Thumb
Geyser Basin

WEST
THUMB

Mount
Sheridan

BRIDGER-TETON NATIONAL FOREST

CENTRAL

PLATEAU

Divide

Information Station
Bookstore

RED
MOUNTAINS

Flagg Ranch

Information Station
Bookstore

Continental

Lewis
Lake

Lewis River

Craig
Pass

Lewis Lake

Lewis Falls

To Jackson

YELLOWSTONE

Gibbon
Falls

Continental

Old Faithful

Kepler
Cascades

Road closed from
early November
to mid-May

South Entrance

Visitor Information Station

JOHN D.
ROCKEFELLER,
JR. MEMORIAL
PARKWAY

89

191
287

Snake River

Fountain Paint Pot

UPPER
GEYSER
BASIN

Firehole River

Shoshone
Lake

PITCHSTONE PLATEAU

GRAND TETON
NATIONAL PARK

Great Fountain Geyser

Midway Geyser Basin

Information Station
Bookstore

Mystic
Falls

Biscuit Basin

Black Sand Basin

Visitor Center

LOWER GEYSER BASIN

Firehole R

Firehole Falls

Mt Haynes

West Entrance

West
Yellowstone

MADISON

WYOMING

IDAHO WYOMING

Gibbon

CORNER

Ouzel Falls

CASCADE

River

Union Falls

Bechler

River

Cave
Falls

Grassy Lake

Road

Road closed
in winter

WYOMING

IDAHO

TARGHEE
NATIONAL
FOREST

APPROXIMATE CALDERA BOUNDARY

PLATEAU

MONTANA
IDAHO

For Further Reading

The nonprofit Yellowstone Association sells books (more than 300 titles), maps, videos, CDs, and other items relevant to Yellowstone and this region at park outlets; by mail at P.O. Box 117, Yellowstone National Park, WY 82190-0117; or via the Internet at www.YellowstoneAssociation.org.

Proceeds of sales benefit park educational programs and services. The National Park Service also publishes reports and other documents about Yellowstone; most are available on the park's website, www.nps.gov/yell. Also visit the National Park Service website at www.nps.gov.

Selected books are:

Anderson, Roger and Carol Shively Anderson. *A Ranger's Guide to Yellowstone Day Hikes*, 2000.

Bryan, T. Scott. *The Geysers of Yellowstone*, 1995.

Consolo-Murphy, Sue and Kerry Murphy. *Wildlife @ Yellowstone: The Story Behind the Scenery*, 1999.

Good, John and Kenneth Pierce. *Interpreting the Landscape: Recent and Ongoing Geology of Grand Teton and Yellowstone National Parks*, 1996.

Haines, Aubrey. *The Yellowstone Story: A History of Our First National Park* (two volumes), 1996.

Henry, Jeff. *Yellowstone Winter Guide*, 1993 (1998).

Janetski, Joel. *Indians of Yellowstone Park*, 1987.

Keiter, Robert and Mark Boyce. *The Greater Yellowstone Ecosystem: Redefining America's Wilderness Heritage*, 1991.

Marschall, Mark, *Yellowstone Trails: A Hiking Guide*, 1999.

McEneaney, Terry. *Birds of Yellowstone*, 1988.

Schullery, Paul. *Searching for Yellowstone: Ecology and Wonder in the Last Wilderness*, 1997 (1999).

Smith, Robert and Lee Siegel. *Windows Into the Earth: The Geologic Story of Yellowstone and Grand Teton National Parks*, 2000.

Whittlesey, Lee and National Park Service staff. *A Yellowstone Album: A Photographic Celebration of the First National Park*, 1997.

Yellowstone Association. *Yellowstone: Official Guide to Touring America's First National Park*, 1998.

Acknowledgments

The National Park Service thanks all those who made the preparation and production of this handbook possible. Special thanks go to the Yellowstone Association, Safari Club International Foundation Sables, and Yellowstone National Park staff. Diane Chalfant, Carolyn Duckworth, and Linda Young of the park staff worked to bring it to fruition. This handbook was prepared by the staff of the National Park Service, Division of Publications: Melissa Cronyn, art director; Nancy Morbeck Haack, cartographer; Mark Muse, production; Tom Patterson, cartographer; Lori Simmons, cartographer; and Ed Zahniser, editor.

David Rains Wallace, who wrote Parts 1 and 2 of this handbook, has been a full-time writer on natural history and conservation topics since 1978. His book *The Klamath Knot* won the John Burroughs Medal for Nature Writing in 1984. In 1990, Wallace received a Fulbright Grant to write a history of Costa Rica's national park system.

Index

Numbers in italics refer to photographs, illustrations, and maps.

☆ GPO: 1999–454-765/00005   Printed on recycled paper.

National Park Service

Picture Sources

Photos and artwork not credited are from the files of Yellowstone National Park and the National Park Service. Most materials may not be reproduced without permission of their owners.

Front cover Larry Ulrich; 2-3 Jeff Foott; 4-5 Jeff Gnass; 6-7 DRK/Stephen J. Krasemann; 8-9 Larry Ulrich; 10-11 Jeff Gnass; 14-15 Willard Clay; 16 Fred Hirschmann; 17 Larry Ulrich; 20-21 Diana Stratton; 22 Gilcrease Museum; 23 Jefferson National Expansion Memorial; 26 Diana Stratton; 27 Jeff Foott; 32-33 Rob Wood/NPS; 33 Robert Hynes/NPS; 34-35 Heinrich Berann/NPS; 36-37 Larry Mayer; 38 Larry Ulrich; 40 George Wuerthner; 42-43 hunt painting by Arthur F. Tait and painted hide, Buffalo Bill Historical Center; 43 stamps, Smithsonian Institution; 44 Hayden Survey Map, National Archives; 44-45 camp and Annie, William Henry Jackson/NPS; 45 surveyor, William Henry Jackson/Denver Public Library; 45 transit and diary, Tom Murphy/NPS; 48 logo, Tom Murphy/NPS; 48-49 F.J. Haynes/Montana Historical Society; 49 touring buses, Burlington Northern & Santa Fe Railroad; 52-53 Raymond Gehman/National Geographic Society; 54-55 Tom Murphy/NPS; 60 William Henry Jackson/Smithsonian Institution; 61 Harlan Kredit/NPS; 62 Art Wolfe; 66-67 Jeff Vanuga; 68-69 Robert Hynes/NPS; 70-71 Diana Stratton; 74-75 Jeff Vanuga; 76-77 illustrations, Robert Hynes/NPS ; 77 researcher, Walt Matell; 80-81 Michael Simon; 82 DRK/Stephen J. Krasemann; 84 fireweed, DRK/John Gerlach; 84 monkeyflower and paintbrush, Erwin and Peggy Bauer; 84 marigold, Jeff Foott; 84 prickly pear, Tom Murphy; 84 phlox, Rob Outlaw; 84 lupines, Diana Stratton; 85 bitterroot, DRK/John Mathews; 85 balsamroot, Carolyn Duckworth; 85 geranium, slipper, and stonecrop, Tom Murphy; 85 star and forget-me-nots, Rob Outlaw; 86 elk, DRK/T. Bledsoe; 86 mountain lion, Jeff Foott; 86 pronghorn, warbler, and grouse, Tom Murphy; 86 blackbird, Diana Stratton; 87 moose, DRK/ Wayne Lankinen; 87 eagle, DRK/Tom and Pat Leeson; 87 swan, pika, and owl, Tom Murphy; 87 badgers and bluebird, Diana Stratton; 88 Raymond Gehman/National Geographic Society; 96-97 Joel Sartore /National Geographic Society; 100 Cupric [perpetually] and Canary, Fred Hirschmann; 101 Punchbowl, Jeff Gnass; 101 [red] and Violet, Fred Hirschmann; 101 Grotto, Tom Murphy; 101 Clepsydra, Larry Ulrich; 102 Grand and Castle, Fred Hirschmann; 102 Carr Clifton; 103 Cliff, DRK/D&P Valenti; 103 Riverside, Jeff Gnass; 103 Old Faithful, Fred Hirschmann; 103 Lion, Glenn Van Nimwegen; 104 F.J. Haynes/Minnesota Historical Society; 108-109 Jeff Vanuga; 110-111 Erwin and Peggy Bauer; 114 Sandra Nykerk; 115 Michael H. Francis; 120 Jeff Foott; back cover Jeff Foott.